Bernard Montpeirous and I became close in 2003 during one of my stays at the Roosevelt Hotel in New York City. I had always known him to be gregarious and personable as the head doorman there. He was also as accommodating to me as a VIP as he was to the other guests. One night I went outside to try a new stogie and we struck up a memorable conversation about the interesting things that could be done with cigars. We have been trading stories ever since.

For me, crazy as it seems, there is a real relationship between wild, reckless abandon off the field and being that way on the field. My reckless abandon on the field has led me to be considered the greatest defensive player in football history. Bernard's life has also been full of wild, reckless abandon on and off his "field". As someone who has let my demons get the best of me at times, I can relate to his stories of complete depravity as well as I can relate to his stories of redemption. When Bernard recounts the story of picking up the phone to speak to his mother in the middle of one of his benders it brings me back to the many times I was brought back to reality when my family reached out to me.

I have been proud to counsel and sponsor Bernard as we both continue on our journeys. Relaying the stories in this book has been as cathartic for Bernard as writing my autobiographies were for me and I think you will see the parallels in our lives. As I tell Bernard all the time, all we can do is be in it to win it.

- Lawrence Taylor

THE REVOLVING DOOR

Chronicles of a New York City Doorman

Bernard Montpeirous

© 2017 Bernard Montpeirous
All rights reserved.

ISBN: 1523920173
ISBN 13: 9781523920174
Library of Congress Control Number: 2017911029
CreateSpace Independent Publishing Platform
North Charleston, South Carolina

The Revolving Door
Memoirs of a Doorman
Written by Bernard Montpierous

What pornography is really about, ultimately, isn't sex but death.
-Susan Sontag

What you have to do is enter the fiction of America, enter America as fiction.
It is, indeed, on this fictive basis that it dominates the world.
-Jean Baudrillard

We can say that the essence of normality is the refusal of reality
-Ernest Becker

1

DOORMAN

A doorman knows things. He knows everyone. He knows no one. He stands, he looks, he drifts, he thinks.

For fifteen years, I've been that doorman. I'm now forty-three years old, a first generation Haitian American, and I guess I'm writing this memoir, if that's what you want to call it, to reveal the decadence and absurdity that I witnessed and participated in during the late nineties while working my first job at Manhattan's illustrious residential Pierre Hotel.

This hotel was top-shelf, vintage New York, forty-three floors of pure regal charm, housing the most elite and famous people in the world. And we broke into so many of these rooms while these people were out of town, and staged unimaginable parties in their homes and got away with it all. I mean, I got a blow job once on Mick Jagger's bed with his blue jeans wrapped around my ankles. I even rubbed one out in Sylvester Stallone's shower, and then blew through a few rails of coke off his kitchen table. And Julia Roberts?

I ate a Twinkie out of a call-girl's ass on her granite floor. What about Pacino and Cosby?

They'd sling me by my throat if they knew about the orgy-train we rode through their living rooms. But we were just kids, service workers, second-class citizens, and we didn't give a damn about these people. To us, *they* had it all.

I don't know why I've waited this long to tell this story now. Back then, I think I was terrified of exposing such a scandalous secret. I just didn't want to go to jail at twenty-eight years old or end up dead in an alleyway. To be honest, though, I don't think I'd be writing this book if I hadn't stumbled upon this crate in my shed. I hardly ever go back there, but last week my wife asked me to pull out our daughter Madison's bicycle. Rifling through this cabinet I found this old, dusty box containing at least a hundred spiral notebooks, all of which documented those debauched couple of years I'd spent at the Pierre.

I sat on a stool and began to flip through the pages of these notebooks. I recognized the handwriting but the voice was so agitated and fragmented that it was almost impossible to read. It was as if a lunatic wrote it. The more I looked at these scribblings, the more I wanted to understand them. These were the golden ruinous days when I drank, fucked and inhaled sheets of cocaine night after night—the kind of pleasure that'll chew your brain raw. This was also right around the time when I met my wife Odie, and when my father died of cancer—but that's a different story, a different book altogether. Do you really want to hear another story about someone dying?

What I'm about to divulge may come across as hollow and self-indulgent, even pornographic at times, but to be fair, I think you should hold back your judgment, because I know I'm not the only one who's been sucked up and deluded by the excesses of this country. It's everywhere—America is the supreme fiction. We buy, eat, fuck, and die. And I bet that most people, if confronted by my identical situation, at that same age, and if they're truly honest with themselves, would have an incredibly difficult time refusing the opportunity I was presented with back then.

Regardless, I'm now interested in pulling back the curtain on my youth, to see why I so willingly gave in to this peculiar kind of destruction and vulgarity. And why we Americans are so fixated on dragging our knuckles through the mud and muck of the rich and famous...

2

LINEN PARADISE

We had the fanciest orgies in New York.
"Open up, it's the police. Open up now," someone shouted, pounding on the front door. Inside, the walls, the floor appeared to move.

"Who the fuck?" I tried to whisper. My dick was soft and the coke had dried up. Beside me were a pair of twins, ginger sisters, all shivers and sobs, crouched naked alongside a baby grand. Black mascara washed their snowy cheeks, and I could see their lips quiver inside the shadow of the piano stool.

Hiro, this Spanish-looking hotel manager, demanded that everyone shut-the-hell-up. "I'll handle it!" Even though this guy was built like a kitten, he could command a room in an instant. He had a voice that forced everyone to listen.

"Open up the door! We know you're in there," someone cried. The thump grew louder.

"Where's Philip? Where's Philip! Where'd he go?" Hiro paced the floor. He dragged his hand through his dark oily hair, wiping drops of sweat from his brow.

But Philip, the assistant manager, was right behind Hiro. He was the party guy who got off teasing his phony mustache and dousing others with hot oil.

The banging on the door persisted. "If you don't open the door we're going to kick this shit down." Coke makes everything appear like it's happening at once. I glared up at the chandelier. It must've have been ten feet long and I almost lost my balance.

"Let's just fucking open it," I thought but didn't say anything.

I'd been to a few of these invite-only soirees but nothing as extravagant. This was linen paradise. Sheets canvassed the entire hotel suite, the floors, the sofas, the chairs, the desks, the tables, the lamps, the televisions, the stereos. It was simple: we didn't want to spill booze or fluids or ash on anything. Everything in these suites was top-dollar. To rent a room cost five grand a night, and most of the guests would hang onto their apartments for months, even years at a time. So if we even scuffed their "home" the slightest, we'd all be swinging by a rope somewhere very far from this feast.

They hammered harder. "We hear you, you sons of bitches. Open up or else we're going to start shooting!"

How did they hear us? The rooms were sound resistant, I thought. And we'd always been so vigilant, picking the suites that took up at least two floors so we could maintain the noise level.

"Hiro, what are we going to do? What are we going to do?" Philip cried.

One night it could be Schwarzenegger's suite, the next night it was Hollywood producer Irwin Winkler's kitchen, and from there we'd wile out in Princess Diana's living room. We'd only break into these places when these people were out of town, working, jetsetting or visiting their second, fourth, or even tenth home. But we all believed that if we rubbed elbows with the fancy, the famous, it just might bring us that much closer to a life worth living.

"Open up the fucking door, you derelicts!"

We never felt guilty about what we were doing, because as first-generation Americans or immigrants we all knew we'd never amount to anything more than doormen, or bellboys, or whatever. So we thought, let's get high and pretend *we're* the kings and queens for the moment: smoking, dancing, drinking, eating, and blowing yards of coke, pummeling each other's bodies, man on man, woman with woman, man eating woman.

"We're going to give you to the count of ten!" This threat was followed by some obstructed laughter.

I shot a glance across the room to a cackling Javier, the Latino elevator kid, draped in a $2000 Egyptian cotton sheet, laced with 22 carat gold. This boy was prancing around like a silly prince. He could've been fourteen years old for all I knew, with those blue eyes and that coffee-colored skin. Now Javier stopped midstride to pour cups of dark chocolate onto Rena's back, while he pulled at himself, his face rippling in mock-agony. Rena, on the other hand, the only black girl among us, with her Jackie O sunglasses, had her face tucked between Holly's legs.

The bartender Jimmy, long and shiny black, darted across the living room, burying himself behind the curtains. This guy had already hit jail twice. He once told me, "The jails in this country are not meant for people like us. We might be poor but we're not criminals."

That was last month's party, right after he'd jerked off into a glass of Louis XIII Cognac.

But everyone here had some story and most of us were too ashamed to tell it. It was better that we remained strangers with each other. The less real things were, the less painful, because if we ever really knew each other it would destroy the game, the illusion.

"You guys are all going away for a long time! That's it we're coming in!" Hiro once again tried to calm everyone down, his chicken arms flapped, his loud black eyes rounded, as he hollered, "Tell Javier shut his mouth, already, and someone turn off the music. Turn off the music!" And that was the first time I noticed that the Nutcracker theme was blaring.

"We'll be one minute. One minute!" Hiro cried through the door. "Just a minute."

I'd never seen Hiro come apart like this. He took out this bullet-shaped thing from his pocket, pushed it up his nose, and gave a quick pull. Philip saw that Hiro was disintegrating and so he also tried to quiet everyone down. Holly looked up in a haze and began stroking Philip's penis. She had the look of a fresh-faced Sharon Stone, hiding behind five coats of blush and foundation. You'd see Holly at every party, but she never once said a word about herself.

"If you don't step away from the door you will be shot!" The person sounded hysterical, possessed.

So how'd we all get here? How were we ever invited to this insanity? No one *ever* asked. We knew better and I suppose for each person it was a different story. If Hiro liked something about you then you were asked to come. And the girls, excluding Holly, were always some brand-new string of beauties. Sometimes they'd come back but Hiro generally liked to change it up and "keep it nice."

"Okay here we go! 10-9-8!" I heard more laughter beyond the door.

Holly moved faster over Philip. "Stop that, stop that," I heard him say, swatting her hand. He didn't like women. Well, not all the time.

Now the cops were just kicking at the door. It sounded like a machine pounding on the wood. "That's it, this shit is coming down!"

"We'll be one minute, I said," Hiro's voice cracked. "We're just organizing stuff, organizing the apartment." The truth was we were just standing there, waiting on the moment.

"7, 6! We're at 6 already, you assholes!"

"We're done," I said to myself. I wanted to call my girlfriend Odie and couldn't. It'd been two months since her miscarriage. And I knew she was in our apartment right then, curled into the covers, trying to forget her life, and here I was in the middle of some salacious orgy, trying to remember how I even got here, wishing I was someone else, somewhere far from all of this.

"You better open that fucking door! 5, 4," someone said, laughing.

I looked around the room at the rest of the crew. We were going to jail. Odie was going to leave me, and my family would never speak to me again.

"We're coming in. 3, 2. You better have your hands where we can see them."

"Let's just open the door," I said. "This is absurd." They all looked at me as a traitor.

"Don't touch it, Bernard," Hiro said, sweat dropped from his forehead onto the sheets below.

I decided to open the door and confront our fate. I wanted to be the hero, but I wanted to be killed in the process, so the people closest to me would pity me one day.

When I finally opened it, I saw that it was just Rocco, the brain of the group, with his movie star good looks. He was leaning inside that door, with that reckless smile, and I just lost it. We both barreled over in laughter, and when I stood up I tackled the bastard and kept punching until someone pulled me off. It was as if I were watching myself, as I threw each jab. The blood surged through my body. I'd been searching for that feeling for a long time. "You stupid guinea prick! What the hell was that? What the fuck is wrong with you? You fucking asshole!" I was crying and didn't know why. The twins under the piano wept, too, and the sheets below them were yellow and wet-looking.

Rocco walked up to me and looked me straight in the face. "You're just a dumb black nigger."

I said nothing. His pretty face looked like a bag of rotten meat, and I didn't care.

Everyone was exhausted and pissed off at Rocco. But once he pulled out some whites to divvy up, well, all was forgiven. I had no interest at that point, my nose was cooked. So I walked over to the smaller twin, the one who looked less confused, with less lipstick, and took her from behind, and immediately I could feel the throb of her insides.

She let off this soft mechanical cry.

We finished up in a few minutes and went out to the balcony to take in the quiet beauty of Central Park. The city lights winked. Traffic made ribbons around the park. She took out this bag of weed. We lit up and blew smoke halos that sailed off to the pavement below.

"Do you think anyone can see us?" she asked.

"I hope so." I looked down at myself, pulsing and red, and then over to her distended nipples. I couldn't go at it again. My body was dried out. I'd already blown my load four times.

"Sometimes I want to disappear, Gerard," she said, and she wouldn't look at me.

"It's Bernard," I corrected her. "Where would you go if you disappeared?" "Somewhere. I don't know, anywhere but here." She rubbed her eyes. "Wow, I'm baked. I'm not sure. Can we not talk about this sort of weird shit right now?"

"Okay. But you brought it up." She looked sad and I wasn't going to ask her why. "Please I said. Please. Here, help me, Gerard." She took my finger and pushed it up her ass. Her face shuddered as if she just downed a bottle of tequila and then my phone rang.

"Who's that?" She had to know. "Who's calling you?" I was surprised she could speak with my finger inside her.

"Just my mother." It was my girlfriend Odie but I didn't want to tell her that.

"She calls you this late?"

"She doesn't sleep that well. She gets nervous about things, everything actually…ever since my dad died."

"Then aren't you going to answer it?"

"No. Not now. I'll call her later."

"Could you love someone like me, Gerard?"

I didn't answer her. I looked down at the park. The smell of smog and industry hung heavy in the air, making all the trees in the park look miserable, and along the sidewalk some tall suit cradled his son over his shoulder. The boy's mother, wearing a long dark dress, trailed behind until they waved a cab. The car stopped, they opened the door and placed the boy in the backseat, and off they went, withdrawing into the noisy sway. I wondered where they were going, what their lives were like. I realized it was now no longer possible to engage in this "good life," the life my family hoped for. And the more I strayed from this idea the less likely I'd find my way back. But I wanted it back. I just didn't know how to get it.

Then I felt someone licking the back of my leg. This girl was insatiable, but I couldn't go for another. When I turned around, I saw that she was passed out on the floor next to me. Yet looking up at me was this Pomeranian pup, with these big brown eyes and a taut red bow twisted about her forehead. I leaned over to pet her when she tore into my hand.

"Fuck you!" I yelled. My voice sang out so big that maybe all of Manhattan heard me. I turned and looked back at the room, a line of bobbing heads in that soft light, a mile-long stare, all laughing at me, and I laughed along. I'm not sure what for.

3

MARCO POLO & AMERICA THE BLOW JOB

After writing that last chapter, I was honestly disturbed by how we violated these people's homes, and how we never got caught. But according to the journals that's how it transpired...

>*Dear America the Blow Job!*
>
>*You're king. But you work so hard. Give props to the hair-flipping grubby eye-work!*
>
>*It's all performance, all theatrics! No love! She doesn't know you. You don't know her. You don't want to know her. She doesn't want to know you. She knows how to make your knees give out. Your eyes roll back. She'll make you smile before you cry. The blow job is what America wants. We'll be dead before we feel anything. She owns you. You own her. You grab at her hair. You put it all the way to the back of her throat. She can bite down whenever she wants to. And then you spill all over her face. Pure music! God = music. Blow jobs = music. Second blow job tonight. I thought the cops showed up. No it was just Rocco fucking with us again. Fucking pretty boy. He pretended he was the fucking police. I punched that asshole till his head was all blood.*

Life is good. America is good. America, America, the ass-tittie capital of the world!
Out on the balcony, had my big thumb up this girl's ass.
Got bit by this dog tonight, that little bitch.

Signed forever,

Bernard Montpeirous

I could never show any of this writing to my wife Odie. She knows some things about my past, what I've told her, but she's not privy to everything. It would ruin her. And if you'd asked me all those years ago, when my head was still a balloon, filled with drivel and drugs, where I thought I might be today, well, it wouldn't be here: the wife, the kid, the car, the house, the job. These days I have to think: How am I even here? I mean, back then, during the old linen days, I was someone else, and now I don't know who I am...

To clear my mind, I took a shower. When I stepped out of the tub, I overheard my nineyear-old daughter's voice rise up to the second story bathroom window. Madison and her new best friend Nicole were splashing in the pool, playing Marco Polo.
"Marco!"
"Polo!"
As I dried off, I heard Odie talking on the phone. Her voice was relaxed and confident, as she dragged on about her boss's bad attitude.
"I don't want to feel underappreciated anymore. I'm the manager there, and I work too hard to get nothing in return," Odie said. I had to look out the window, to see what was going on.
Outside, empty blue skies spread ahead, and down below Madison dove for her friend, a splash flowered in her wake. Her russet curls were flattened by the water, those apple-shaped cheeks scrunched-up as her eyes were shut for the game. Odie was rolled out on a lounge

chair in a blonde summer dress. Her long brown golden hair dressed her neck, while she twirled a glass of pinot.

"He knows no one likes him. He does it to himself," Odie said, maybe.

Though, I couldn't really hear everything she was saying, because a few houses down someone started banging on a drum set, and each time she would try to speak, this "drummer" would attack the kit. The pounding would start and stop, circling back, only to begin again. It was this playful, broken beat that I couldn't stop listening to.

After a few minutes, maybe longer, I tuned back into what Odie was saying, "I heard Donna is going to confront him Monday morning about it. If she doesn't then I will. Jesus, do you hear that racket in the background? A racket, I said. It sounds awful. My god. You don't hear that crap? It's like tribal crap or something." She raised her voice. "Well, anyway, I think someone should step up to the plate and say something to him already. It's only going to get worse."

Hearing her speak made me glad, a sort of gladness that goes unnoticed most days because it's constant. Odie always seems to be in the moment, despite our hellish past together, those dark years I'd pushed to her human limit, and now somehow, everything has been forgotten. She refuses to acknowledge the past.

"Well, what do you think? Am I wrong? Do you *hear* those damn drums? Or am I going crazy? You don't hear them? I can't even think straight. Yeah, but he's just not fair to anyone," Odie said, as she fiddled with that silver bracelet around her wrist, something she's worn since the first day I met her.

Madison and Nicole continued to kick and splash, when Odie cupped her hand over the receiver and cried out, "Honey, don't splash so much. You're going to knock all the water out of the pool."

Not hearing or maybe not acknowledging her mother, Madison seemed even more inspired to catch her snaking friend. "Marco!" she shrilled.

"Polio! Polio! Polio!" Nicole responded, diving from Madison's lunge.

"Marco, Marco, Marco!" she plunged into the water, slapping Nicole's eye.

Odie continued to talk on the phone, "Where are you going on vacation this year? Oh. Nice. I still have to discuss it with Bernard, to see what he's thinking now. Last week, I think he said he wanted to go to Haiti to see his family but I want to go to Italy. Haiti just seems so depressing these days. Hold on Diane. Madison's friend is crying." She stood up.

"What happened?" she asked Madison.

"Mom, I hit her eye. But it was by accident."

Nicole covered her eye. "It hurts! It hurts!" she cried.

"Let me see it. Let me see your eye," Odie said.

Standing at the window, watching my family swooped up by the pleasures of another lazy summer afternoon, I thought: *This isn't my life.* I mean, this is my body, these are my hands, my feet, sure, but all of this seems more than real. It's as if I'm watching myself participate in this life, and everything seems as delicate as a dream. How could the 'Bernard' at those linen parties be the same person standing right here? When Odie hung up the phone, she called out: "Bernard!"

I didn't answer.

"Bernard, are you there!"

"I'll be right down!" I said.

"Bernard, what is all that banging! You need to go over and tell whoever's making that racket to stop making that racket. It's driving me nuts. And Bernard, are you coming down! I want to go to Home Depot before we go to dinner. Bernard? Are you listening to me?"

"I'm coming!"

I can't help but think: *I don't deserve this.* There shouldn't be a loving wife or a smiling child. I should be somewhere else. Not here. And sometimes I want to be somewhere else, someone else. Not here on the placid shores of Long Island, coddled by the ordinary, the expected. No, I should be somewhere else. Maybe in some dirt bar with my fat fingers wrapped around another cheap beer, another woman whose name I won't have to remember in the morning. I shouldn't be this lucky, because when I came back from that party, the night that vile dog bit me, it should've been the last time I saw Odie. I was dead wrong then, and none of this should be here.

So I'm not sure if I should tell you about that morning when I came home to Odie's delirious fists, right after that damn dog bit me, or maybe I'll just explain what happened that first year at the Pierre leading up to that moment…

4

THE PIERRE & 30,000 HAITIANS SLAUGHTERED

I remember that first day working the door, well, some of it at least. I was young, naïve, hoping to impress anyone who'd listen, and maybe that's why I got this job in the first place. Or it could've been because I spoke some French, and having a French doorman at a French hotel made sense. Never mind that I'm Haitian, when Hiro introduced me to the rest of the staff, he always said, "This is Bernard Montpeirous, our newest *French* doorman." It felt good to have this identity, to hear my name said out loud. When I first tried on that top hat and mink-fur collared coat with those soft white gloves, I felt important, with a renewed purpose.

Hiro ushered me through the building. Each floor had more gold and glass and silk and marble than the previous. Everything was shiny, exuding luxury and importance.

"You'll get the hang of this place in no time," Hiro said.

"Okay," I said, but I was overwhelmed by what I saw.

And before I could button my shirt to the top, I went into the bathroom and called my parents from a stall to tell them the great news.

"Dad? Hey, guess what? I got the job! I got it. They gave me this hat. I got this coat, too. You're talking to the Pierre Hotel's newest doorman."

"That's fantastic news." He sounded proud, and this must've been right around the time when he first got sick, when the cancer was supposed to be "manageable."

"Even the toilets here are made of gold, Dad."

"Just make sure you smile with every one of your teeth, Bernard. That's how the tips happen. Here, let me put your mother on. She needs to hear this too." I have to admit I never felt I'd measured up to what my parents expected of me.

How could I? They were both raised as Haitian bourgeois. My mother lived in a palace with servants. They had lavish parties and traveled all the time. Her grandfather, my *great* grandfather, Sylvain Salnave, was the president of Haiti in the nineteenth century until he was assassinated by his own government. Eventually, all of this old money dried up. Then in the 1960's, my mother was actually imprisoned by President Papa Doc Duvalie for her association with this bourgeois class.

Duvalie was the infamous tyrant who implemented "the brain drain," which resulted in the slaughter of 30,000 "unfit" Haitians. When my mother was finally released, she fled the island and found her new home in Queens, New York, where she had to start all over.

Because of this countrywide unrest, my father also sought refuge in Queens. Two weeks after arriving in America, and in somewhat fairytale fashion, my parents met and married. I don't know the exact details of their romance but apparently it was immediate, and of course they didn't wait too long to have both me and my sister Isabella. To this day, my mother refuses to bring up what happened back then. I've asked her a few times through the years, but she never gives a straight answer. I only know a little about my family's history because of what other family members, uncles and aunts and cousins, have told me along the way.

Anyway, I was in the stall, and my father kept at it: "You'll make a great doorman.

I'm sure of it."

"Thanks, Dad." Just as every child will forever think there are monsters under their bed, they'll also always perceive their fathers to loom larger than they actually do.

Nevertheless, that day, when I heard the old man's voice brim with genuine satisfaction, I could picture his mellow white smile, and for that fleeting moment I could relax being his son.

"Here, let's put your mother on," he said.

I heard the phone rustle and the old man call out my mother's name, when someone walked into the bathroom and stepped into the stall next to mine just as my mother got on the line. "Bernard, I just heard. I just heard your father talking. My son's going to be working at the *Pierre Hotel*." What interests me today is how proud they were when I got the job, because it wasn't like I was asked back into royalty. I was only offered the opportunity to *work* for the royal class at a ritzy hotel. Maybe my parents thought it would bring me that much closer to their old bourgeois way of living or maybe they were just happy that I was happy.

"Thanks Ma. Thanks. Okay, Ma, I have to go Ma. I have to get back to work," I whispered.

"Why are you whispering?"

"I'll call you later. I can't talk now."

"Why can't you talk? Is something wrong?"

"I'll call you later, Ma."

Compared to my "royal" parents, I guess at that point I'd always considered myself as a failure, after having dropped out of five different colleges, and with no real career prospects, but this new job saved my life, or at least it did so in my mind. In hindsight, now that I'm a parent myself, I'm sure my parents only wanted the best for me, and perhaps my worry about not meeting their standards was just a buckling of the truth.

"I love you, Bernard."

"Love you too, Ma."

I often wish I had a recording of that conversation just so I could listen to it over and again. If I try hard enough I can call back their voices. The easiness in their inflection, something you take for granted while you're young, when you don't realize how simple things were. And how much of that simplicity is a result of your parents' devotion, a distraction from the brute-realism which awaits even the most fortunate. It's only after they pass, like my father, that you recognize how much of your well-being was hinged upon their affection.

5

STRANGERS WITH NAMES & ORGY TRAINS

After a few weeks at the Pierre, I got a sense of what kind of place this hotel was—or at least the kind of crowd it attracted. This was the dot-com boom, prior to Reality-TV and paranoia 9-11, before the big banks crumbled—the Clinton years, when America was that careless king, when the tips still rolled in. And the residents here were the "beautiful people." They had more money than they could spend, many of whom owned entire floors, duplexes, and sometimes even three floors. Suites with sixteen rooms, five master bedrooms, seven bathrooms, twenty-three-foot-high ceilings, and terraces that wrapped around sweeping views of Central Park.

As the doormen here, we were supposed to cater to this elite group. They were "gods," which required being a specialist at the job. You couldn't flub a thing because the hotel often hired a company of professional spotters who'd pop in every so often, feigning they were customers, just to make sure everyone followed the strict hotel protocol: greeting the clients, carrying the luggage, opening the doors, collecting tips, etc.

"You've got to look everyone right in the eye with that big smile, Bernard," Hiro would remind me, and I listened to every directive no matter how bold or condescending.

"Stand up straight. Straighter."

"Only two suitcases at a time, Bernard."

There was no excuse but to perform perfectly, and it was understood that once you were "in" at this coveted hotel you did your best to stay. However, sometimes even an honest effort wasn't enough, as people were let go all the time and without any explanation.

Yet some workers lasted on this job for twenty, thirty, sometimes even forty years.

"They let go of Manny," Jimmy mentioned one day after work. Rocco, Jimmy, and I were shoving off to the dive down the block for a drink.

"Why?" I asked.

"Because he's a clammy, corpulent bastard, that's why," Rocco said.

"What does that even mean?" Jimmy asked.

"He's fat and he's sweaty, Jimmy. America hates fat people, Jimmy. Have you ever seen a fat star?"

"A fat star?" Jimmy asked.

"A fat movie star, Jimmy. A celebrity."

I interrupted, "Yeah, how about John Candy?"

"Don't interrupt me, dog-dick. I'm speaking, and that was the flipping eighties anyhow. Nothing good ever emerged from the eighties. I'm talking about an authentic celebrity like right now, someone with unopposed credibility like Brad Pitt or Johnny Depp.

Do you think they'd be worth a goddamn nickel if they were fat-asses?"

"Manny wasn't fat," I said.

"Whatever you want, B. It's all yours." Rocco walked faster, and we tried to keep up the pace.

"I just don't think he is," I said. "He's a little bigger than some of us but he's not fat."

"Can we end this conversation? You're compromising my buzz, dog-dick," Rocco said.

"Why do you keep calling me that?" I asked.

"Do I have to explain why I call you *dog-dick*, dog-dick?" I never understood why he called me that. To most people at the Pierre, I didn't have a name. I was only known as the "French" doorman with the nice smile.

I suppose one of the hardest parts about working that door was being *no one*, preserving anonymity while dealing with the guests. Because hotel policy stated that you were to treat the residents as untouchables, strangers with names. Naturally, there was always someone "fantastic" spiraling through those glass doors: "Good day, Mr. Jagger.

Nice to you see, Mrs. Fairfax." And it didn't matter if it was Madonna and her fabulous entourage or Robert De Niro's cordial handshake or Michael Jackson and his bodyguards or just Bob Dylan tumbling home at 4AM, whistling one of his three-chord ditties, you were prohibited from engaging with these guests on any personal level. You knew their money, how much they tipped, and that was it.

"Sir, my bags are over there."

"I'll take that bag for you, Ms. Winfrey."

"Can you not carry it like that?"

"Of course, Mr. Tyson. Will you need anything else, Mr. Tyson?"

This was a temporary home for most guests, where they could rid themselves of "real life," or at least the responsibility of it. There was an obvious freedom in residing in a place stripped of any emotional attachment. Residents were strangers, stacked in this gilded high-rise, breathing, eating, merrymaking, in the seclusion of their luxury, all small gestures and big money. And there was something untouchable about them, and maybe that's the reason they became "successful" in the first place, because of their ability to *never* let their guard down.

"I need a cab."

"Yes, Ma'am, right away."

It wasn't too long after, maybe four or five months on the job, that I was invited to my first Pierre linen party. For some reason, I was the only doorman ever invited. Hiro told everyone that I had a "good smile" and would be a "good fit" for the crew.

But yeah, one day while working the door, Hiro just walked up to me and said, "You should meet me after work, I have something important to go over with you." I had no idea what he was talking about but I listened.

We met in his office and told me: "Just be there at 10PM sharp and don't expect to leave until 7AM."

"Okay." I'm still not sure today why Hiro asked me out of everyone who worked there. I often wonder how different my life would've turned out if I hadn't had that "good smile."

"And don't come empty-handed," Hiro said. By which he meant: bring Vicodin,

Quaaludes, pot, coke, or whatever.

So the parties began, and by this point the crew had become experts in flipping these rooms. It was a pseudo-art. The sheets, the booze, the ladies, and all we had to do was say some mindless code word to the elevator boy, something relative to the suite we were breaking into that night (ex: Rocky 4, Like a Virgin, etc.) and within minutes we'd be sliding up to what would be the rudest celebration anyone had ever seen. And each party was rarer, more outrageous than its predecessor. The higher we got, the more we screwed and the more we wanted to obliterate our past, our homes, our failures, and our second-rate lives.

And I dove into these carnal-outings with no inhibitions. "You sick fuck, Bernard!" Javier said. He couldn't believe I ate a Twinkie out of a girl's ass. He looked too happy for his own good. "But you're my fucking hero, man. Holy shit!" he said. Thinking about all this now, I don't know whether to laugh or have a full-on panic attack.

I mean, one night, we'd dressed up in oversized animal costumes. The next time we'd paint each other with glow-in-the-dark paint. There was Vegetable Night, which ranged from apples to zucchini, all lodged into every orifice possible. Followed by naked pillow fights, all-night dance marathons, golden showers, Cops and Robbers, Cowboys and Indians, Mailman and Mr. Doggie, the Sex Olympics, orgy trains. But no one ever questioned any of this nonsense. We just went along with the gag, waiting for the "lights" to be turned on, hoping it'd never happen, hoping we'd stay young forever.

What's still perplexing about this, though, is that these so-called educated elite had no idea about the moonshine that went on in their rooms. I think our crew was just that artful in cultivating a respectable persona, so cunning that the Pierre guests always felt confident they were receiving a five-star service. And I'd heard that Hiro only had to answer to a few of the owners, and they were hardly ever around to check up on him, and for some reason they trusted him.

I think we might have missed once, when this cleaning lady caught the crew shuffling into Madonna's room. That was easy, though. Hiro roped her in to the party that night, and I think he even handed this woman a few hundred bucks, convincing her to allow him to take her from behind, and she even let him pull on her hair a little. And I could tell that lady was more than thankful than upset. "My God, my God, my God, my God," she repeated, over and again. Hiro looked over at me while he kept at it, giving the crew two thumbs up. It was his belief that *"Everyone* has the animal buried within. You just have to know how to drag it out."

But now that I think about it, I don't remember seeing that lady around the building after that. Maybe she quit or was she fired? People were constantly rotating in-and-out at the Pierre, never hanging around long enough to remember who they were.

6

MS. PIGGY, SUICIDE & PEACOCK HATS

It was sometime in April, nearly a year into the job, and it must have been right around the time when my father spent his last month tied to his death bed. Anyway, I'm digressing, but at that point, I was a year into working that Pierre door, and had become good at my job. I had most of the tricks of this cracked gig down pat, and I was partying all the time. But yeah, this one afternoon I'll never forget: it was deep navy skies and work was dead, as I drifted at my post, replaying the details of the previous night's bash through my head. Wherever my eyes wandered along the avenue, I'd imagine some absurd sexual feat. There was always a flood of imagery to draw upon during those drawn-out feverish bouts. So I'd stop to marvel as the crew went at it, bodies colliding, while shrieking holy-hell.

Though for some reason that day I couldn't get this one image out of my head: a lanky almond-eyed girl who I popped the lid on a few times. She begged me to tear into her on this kitchen table, pronging her with this old diamond-studded rotary telephone, which was probably worth ten grand. She also demanded I call her "Ms. Piggy," because it was one of the names one of her boyfriends called her. After a couple of rounds of squealing, I understood why I should fold to her wishes.

And just as Ms. Piggy was about to climax again in my daydream, I was interrupted by this harrowing whistle from above as someone

THE REVOLVING DOOR

hollered and kicked his way down five stories to a quiet thud on the pavement in front of me. His body scattered, contorted in various directions, a trace of blood chased back to this boyish expression. His name was James or John, Room 509. Forty-two or forty-five years old, who knows? Apparently, this guy had been holed up in his room for a full month, cutting through a stable of hookers and a year's worth of pure Molly. This poor bastard's wife had fled a couple of weeks ago. She met a better man, I was told, leaving him to rust and wander the city alone. And a few days after this incident, Rocco or Javier informed me that this man used a kitchen knife to carve the words "EMPTY" into his left calf right before he made his decision to descend into oblivion.

When I ran up to the man's body, he was already gone, the air around him swallowed by silence. I wanted to cry but I didn't want anyone to see me. My breath echoed. The blood lifted through my body. I'd never seen a dead man before, let alone a suicide. I looked up toward the street as everything seemed to stretch with time: the gloss of a Lexus, a cab door jutting open, a patch of sky, a scant streak of cloud, the corroded wing of a gargoyle perched on its ledge. A young father hurried down the block carrying his pigtailed daughter over his shoulder, a strident voice breaking with distance, when everything at once came into focus, "real-time" resumed again. Then the ambulance, the police, screamed up to the entrance where a crowd had met about the body. And I'm sure the surrounding people were thanking whatever God they did or didn't believe in, that it wasn't them this time, they hadn't been hurled into the great-blue-nothing.

Within seconds the emergency crew had Mr. 509 on a gurney, and off they went, red-white lights whipping around the corner. It was okay for the rest of us to go forward with the predictable part of our days. But Hiro remained in the street, only feet from where the scrambled corpse lay. He had the appearance of a boxer who just lost a big fight, his hands roped behind his back. I'd never seen him like this. He was sad. I looked back down the block and police had already begun to line the avenue with yellow tape. When I turned back to Hiro, he flaunted this iridescent blue peacock hat, with his bruise-red lipstick, as he rode this blonde cocktail waitress from behind, his ass cheeks flapping like an old flag in the wind. That's when I remembered what my father once told me: "Death should be treated with grave care."

I walked closer. "Hiro?" I asked.

"Yeah, Bernard."

"You okay?"

"Fine. Get back to work," he said, wiping a tear away.

That's the thing with this job—you're not allowed to be sad. Sad doesn't sell, and the moment you begin to act like a person with real feelings, well, "you better turn that nonsense off."

"Are you sure?" I looked down at the body and thought about this poor bastard's family, only a phone call away, the horror and hell to come. What can you say knowing it's their son or brother or friend? I looked up, a thick haze skimmed over the sun, and I could hear the crowded cries of the bar down the block. It was probably some home-run or nohitter or whatever.

"Bernard, what the hell did I just say? Get back to your post," Hiro said, raising his voice.

I had to go back to the door. Hiro had an unchallenged authority over who went to what fuck-party, and I wasn't going to forgo that.

As soon as I got back to the door I had to run to the bathroom, where I sat on the bowl, crying into my hands. For how long I don't know. But that would be the last time I'd cry for a long time, and I'd be a liar if I said that jumper's face didn't hang in my mind for the rest of that afternoon, the rest of the week. Everywhere I turned it was that same awful stunned expression as if the whole world was some ill-planned joke.

7

CHARLES OSGOOD, MRS. DAVIS & THOSE DAMN DRUMS

Sunday morning, family breakfast. Madison had begged for pancakes. So we sat down to some fresh juice and silver dollars, and watched CBS Sunday Morning with Charles Osgood was on.

"I thought I told you about that suicide jumper years ago," I said.

"I would've remembered something that awful," Odie replied.

"I don't know how you stayed in that industry all these years."

"Not all hotels are like the Pierre. The Roosevelt isn't like that. The people I work with now are good people."

"So wait, you went back to work the next day after that happened?"

"I think so. Probably. I don't know."

"That's just weird. And your parents didn't say anything about this?"

"I don't even know if I told them. My father was dying at that point. I don't know. I just didn't talk about it with anyone. Why do you care?"

Odie interjected. "Oh, stop, Bernard. I hate when you get like this."

"Like what?"

"Like this. I don't know what *it* is. The way you're acting now. Like how 'Bernard' acts."

"I don't know what you're talking about."

"You know..." Odie put her fork down, looking toward the window. "It's back.

They're back." She looked empty and angry. "I can't believe they're back."

"What's back?"

"Those damn drums. Tell me you don't hear that?"

I now heard banging, too. "I'm going to put it louder." I reached for the remote control. "I can't hear what he's saying now," I said.

Odie turned toward Madison and said, "When you finish your pancakes, sweetie, go upstairs and pick out a book that we can read together."

I put the volume up, and the TV blurted, "Not only will drone technology be implemented for military use, but there will soon be eyes in the sky all over the US."

"What'd he just say? Eye in the sky or something?" Odie asked. "Madison, are you eating your waffles?"

"Pancakes, Mom," Madison said, as she tried to tap along with drum beat. "Pancakes, right. Eat your pancakes, sweetie. Bernard, put it louder?" I raised the volume, again. "I thought we'd figured out a long time ago that wars don't work for anyone? Why do we keep doing the same thing over and over again?"

"Because we forget?"

"Damnit, Bernard, I can't hear a thing. What'd he say? I can't hear anything over that noise."

"I don't know what he said. But it all looks like a video game to me."

"It's not a video game. It's a nightmare. These 'video games' actually kill people. It's absolutely absurd. You might as well turn off the TV. I can't hear it anyhow. Bernard, you need to go over there right now and say something. It's been three weeks since you said you would take care of this," Odie said.

"Mom, can we change the channel? The news is so boring. And Mom, Lisa's mom is taking her to the mall today. And I want to go, too. Lisa's mom is getting Lisa a cell phone. Can I get a cell phone today, too?"

"Madison, one minute, honey," Odie said, without looking at her. "Bernard?"

"What do you want me say?" I asked.

"How about that it's nine thirty on a Sunday morning?"

"And how does that matter? People can do whatever they want at this time. I don't even notice it anymore. Does it really bother you all that much?"

"So you're asking me to go over there myself?"

"Fine then I'll go."

Walking toward the clamor, I came upon the house, a vinyl-siding ranch, which looked like every other on this block. They're simply rows of houses, faces, shadows, behind curtains, and it's only when I spot someone that I realize how removed I am from all of them. I want to be friendly with my neighborhood, and I imagine the feeling is mutual; it's just I don't know how to strike up a conversation. "How's your day going?" "Nice car." "Blue skies, eh?" "See the game last night?" So we look at each other, and sometimes there's the occasional wave or quick hello, or even a few pleasantries exchanged, but then we're on our way,

As I got closer to the house, a young brunette in a sweat suit and pony tail pushed her way out of a mini-van parked in the driveway. She looked tired. She slid open the backdoor and pulled out an infant's car seat. The baby was asleep, and I knew at that moment that I had no interest in provoking this new mother. Then she turned toward me, bracing the car seat, squinting like she knew me. I went to say hello when she spun around, zipping into the house. That's when I decided to go home, but I circled the block two extra times, so I could delay having to deal with Odie.

On my way back, I saw my next door neighbor, Mrs. Davis, who was standing on her front lawn, again, looking at nothing, a habit she'd acquired the day her husband died of pancreatic cancer last year. Her skin and eyes gray, she looked like she was waiting to die herself.

I waved to her and then she called me over. "Do you mind giving me a hand, Johnny?

I can't do what I used to," she said.

I couldn't say no to her. We went inside to fix her TV.

"It was just playing a minute ago," she said. "And I'm missing all my shows, right now. This is really terrible, Tommy." Her house was littered with old photos and knickknacks. There was a heavy stench like a hospital lingering in the room.

"I see. It's Bernard, by the way." I pressed the remote's power button and the TV flashed on. Where am I, I thought.

"Oh, thank you, thank you, thank you, Brainard. There should be more people on this earth just like you. You know, I'm not handy at all. My husband was handy, I guess. When he wasn't drunk, that is. So you want a cookie, now, Bobby? I've made some cookies for you."

"No, thank you, Mrs. Davis." I said, grabbing my stomach. "I've had too many cookies in my life."

"But you need to eat, Bobby." She opened the refrigerator, and I was about to ask her if she heard those drums ever, when she asked, "Why are my glasses in the refrigerator? You people should know that they're my glasses. Not yours, you terrible, terrible people."

I walked outside without saying goodbye, and felt bad about it.

When I walked through our front door, I told Odie I spoke with the people about the noise level.

"What'd they say?" she asked.

"They said they'd try to be more conscientious," I said.

"They'd *try* to? Who was playing them?"

"I didn't ask. There's a couple that lives there. A young mom and her baby and a guy, too. They probably have a teenager or maybe it's the guy who plays. I don't know. I didn't ask. I didn't want to bother them anymore."

"You didn't ask? And you didn't want to bother *them*?"

"No, I didn't ask."

8

COCAINE, OLD LADIES & LIZARDS

The night after I sobbed in that stall, after that man jumped to his death, Mickey, a veteran doorman, and I picked up a bag from this guy we knew who stopped by the hotel every now and then. We decided to hit up The Irish Pub on 54th to scout out the ladies. When I went out those days it was always with someone from work, anyone who was interested in having a good time. Most of my friends from when I was younger had vanished. They grew up, I suppose, whether they went away to college, got hitched, had children, moved out of state, or most times they were just absorbed by their careers. But I never saw any of them after high school. They forgot me and so I them. The few who tried to revive old bonds, well, usually within a few weeks we'd realize it wasn't a good idea. The simplicity of our past turned out to be too hard to recreate.

But yeah my friend Mickey had a wife and two kids home, something he liked to crow about whenever we went out. He'd show me pictures of his "beautiful family," and I'd often wonder if his family thought of him in that same way.

"You've got a good-looking family, Mick." I'd say.

The bar stunk of chlorine that night and it was dark, mobbed with faces we knew, names we didn't, all dressed the same: tube tops, jeans, hair gel, and tweezed eyebrows. Toward the end of his life, my father once said that America had lost its imagination, and that everyone now was as pretty as a woman. Nowadays, I'd have to agree with him, but we were on the chase that night and a lay was a lay.

Mickey pointed to this one woman, who waddled in with something wedged inside her ass. "I wouldn't hit that girl with your mom's dick, B," he said.

"You're not going to touch my mother's dick, asshole." We put most of our shift's pay on that bar.

"You want a shot, B?"

The rest of the evening we burned through that bag and shot after shot, blathering on about every one of our co-workers and their infinite flaws. It seemed the more intoxicated we became the more we'd attack everyone else. And Mickey really pushed it all night. He was raw with hate. It was because earlier that day Rocco had teased Mickey about his poor taxi-whistling skills. When the rest of the Pierre crew found out they soon joined in on the torment.

"I can whistle like a motherfucker. Fuck those assholes. They don't know shit about shit," Mickey told me.

"I know it," I said, although I honestly never heard him whistle.

"Here watch. Look at my shit. Here, look at my shit. Look at my lips." He tried but out came air and shame. "You hear that shit, right?" He tried once more.

"I think so but it's loud in here, Mick. But I think I heard it. You've got a good whistle."

"Hey, you hear Lopez got fired?"

"No? He was fired? For what? Wait, who's Lopez? I don't know Lopez."

"Night-shift, guy. Danny Lopez. I don't know why they axed him," he smiled. "He probably deserved it. That fucker was always wandering away from the door. So I hear."

I'm just glad it's not my ass on the curb."

"Yeah, I guess you're right."

"Ah, fuck it, fuck everyone. Right? Here's to the dead man on the sidewalk!" Mickey announced. He raised his glass over his head and I followed, bringing mine up as high as I could. And all I could think of were my parents and what they would've thought if they heard any of this. My old man was bedridden by this point, and my mother was more than likely at his side, gripping what was left of him.

"Here's to the suicide jumper's family and their miserable lives!" he said.

"Here's to getting laid!" I said.

"Here's to the dead man not getting laid!"

"Here's to getting your dick sucked nice and good!"

"Here's to America and the dead man not getting his dick sucked ever again!"

"Here's to drinking shots!"

"Here's to drinking shots and getting laid and getting your dick sucked in America!"

We soon tucked into the bathroom stall and finished the rest of the bag when I noticed I had ten dollars left, good for two more drinks. Though we never made it that far because within minutes of when we got back to our stools, some old hag, who had enough gold around her neck to sail around the world for the next few centuries, demanded that we leave at once, well, as soon as Mickey began running his jaw with her.

"Lady, you look like a lizard, now, don't you," Mickey said. She was leaned over a martini glass. And as soon as Mickey had a few down the hatch, he'd jump into any conversation along the bar. He often said talking with strangers gave him some odd comfort because they couldn't judge him.

"Excuse me, young man?" she asked.

"He didn't say anything," I interrupted. "It was nothing important."

"I said you got the face of a spiny lizard, lady," he slurred, nearly knocking over his drink. I felt sorry for him. Then I felt sorry for me.

"I thought that's what you said. You stay right there, you sonofabitch," she said, finishing her drink.

"Please, don't listen to him. He's not well. His mother passed away this morning." I had to make something up because the truth seemed inadequate.

"We'll be here waiting, lady, and with drink in hand." He waved his glass though the air, pretending to surrender to this woman.

"Why'd you say that, man?" I asked.

"Oh, relax. She's not going to remember anything tomorrow anyway. It's all one big joke anyway, B. None of this shit is real. Look, you think this is really wood?" He tapped the bar with his fingers to prove his point. "That ain't wood. Everything is fake, amigo. You can do whatever the fuck you want, right? If we can drop bombs on countries, B, for example Hiroshima, Japan, and everyone can still forget, then this little old lady getting called a lizard is as harmless as a little wind in the eye."

When I turned around on my stool, the lady was already at the back of the room, stamping her foot, hands flailing, in front of this bulbous Irish-looking bouncer.

Mickey and I didn't budge until that big-ass mick and his buddy came over and escorted us out. And we kicked the whole way to the exit.

"Here's to the good old lady with the martini!" I howled as they dragged me out to the curb, dropping my glass to the floor. The light was bright outside, everything was sharp and distorted.

"Here's to the martini lady with cobwebs in her crotch!" Mickey said.

I don't know how I made it back to my apartment, but I woke up next to some other old lady that I'd never seen before and I was late for work. She was right in my face, her skin was caked in this carrot-colored makeup, which was stretched and stitched, giving her the appearance of a woman twenty years younger. Her hands were as crooked as sticks, bones tied up in wrinkles.

The room looked as if it were turned over by a thief as the sun broke through the blinds. I threw on a shirt and some pants and tried to be polite, asking her to leave in a voice that felt forced. "I'm sorry, Ms. I'm late for work."

"That's okay, Bernard. I can stick around and clean up the apartment and make dinner for us."

She was wrapped in my robe, and I could see her shriveled breasts, which reminded me of a child's fingertips after a bath.

"I think you should go, Ms."

"Okay, do you want a quick bump before you go? I'm going to take one."

She took out her bag, her mirror, and leveled a few lines, and it was all gone before I could even say yes.

"You sure you don't want a taste? I have more," she said I was already ten minutes late. She ripped two more lines.

"I'm sorry, you're going to have to leave."

"You're not being nice, young man. You don't just screw a lady and send her to the streets. I'm not your coke-slut."

"I don't know who you are, honestly. Now, I don't want you to take offense, but I'm late for work. I'm sure we had a great time."

"Fine, I'll leave, Bernard."

She picked up her belongings, walked toward me and then pressed a wet kiss on my lips, tasting of cigarettes and lemons.

"I'll call you later, Bernard." She kept saying my name. I wanted her to go away forever.

"I won't be here later."

"Then I'll call you tomorrow."

I opened the door for her and wanted to puke.

She turned and smiled. "Aren't you going to ask me my name, Bernard?"

"To be honest, I don't want to know your name."

"Oh, kiss my hairy tit, you asshole. I hope I gave you AIDS last night."

I shut the door and ran into the bathroom. My bowels gave out and I almost shit all over the floor. I called Hiro from the bowl and told him my cousin died and that I wouldn't be in to work today. First he offered his deepest condolences. Then he told me to get my lying-ass in to work.

New York can be as cold and strange as they say it is, and if you don't give in to it, well, good luck.

9

AMERICAN DREAMING & DAD'S TAXI

My parents always told me how they had to push along like everyone else in this "land of opportunity." My mother was a high school English teacher, and she could speak English better than most Americans I knew, and my father hustled his whole life as a city taxi driver. In America, they were no longer part of that elite class. Instead, they were middleclass immigrants, humbled by the tyrannical Haitian world that forced them to abandon their prior lives, and yet somehow they maintained their happiness, happy to be alive, happy to have a family, even it required huddling into a tiny two-bedroom apartment in some strange city known as Forest Hills, Queens.

Throughout those early years, though, they did all they could to give us a good life, and they made sure we worked just as hard to keep it. Though I think privately my parents held out hope that one day we'd all return "home," or at the very least our family would reclaim its "throne." And when I think of my mother, the perfectionist she was, I realize, she only expected the best out of her children. According to her, Isabella and I were *required* to go to church every week, to stand up straight, to speak only when spoken to, and to act polite under all circumstances, and there was no TV in the Montpeirous household. Though my mother might come across as strict, it was not because she was selfserving or sadistic, rather she wanted to "enrich our lives," and offer "the life she had," as she'd often put it.

"Bernard, you're to finish your homework before you go outside."

"Can't I finish it later, Ma?"

"I'm not going to answer that. Do you want me to call your father?"

Yet I don't remember seeing my father all that much because he worked all the time. He'd sweat it out six days a week, twelve-hour days, and you'd never hear him grumble a word about his day. It wasn't until I was ten years old, when he first asked me to join him on one of his weekend shifts, that I got a sense of his routine. From that moment forward, every weekend for a few years, I would ride alongside him in his rickety front seat, helping with the luggage, collecting the tips, and he'd say, "Bernard, you've got to smile your way into the hearts and pockets of every customer."

The old man always insisted that I was a "natural born businessman," something he'd repeat over and again to anyone who'd listen, whether speaking to a customer or even our family over a holiday dinner. So maybe I got this "gift" from the old man himself? To be honest some of my clearest memories stem from that front seat of his, and it's only now that I realize how influential those initial father-son moments were.

"One day you're going to do great things, Bernard. You're not going to do what I do," he'd say.

"What things?"

"You'll just do something better. Things will be the way they used to be a few years back."

"But what things, Dad?"

"Don't ask questions. Just listen to your father."

So I grinned and pulled out every suitcase from that dusty trunk, baffling the adults with my unusual strength, lifting bags without a misstep. I made my father proud, and he made me feel important as the streets teemed with people, everyone wild with pursuit, while he would wave his invisible wand over those pulsing city lights, and we would fly through the city, weaving down the avenues, his voice warm and resonant, guiding me along: "You're going to be my co-pilot, today. This is New York, the capital of the world, where everything happens. If you look over there, you can see the Twin Towers. They're some of the tallest, most beautiful buildings in the world."

"I like the one on the left, Dad," I said. I had no preference but even as a boy I felt the need to impress my father, sharing his interests. If my father thought something was "beautiful" then I'd have to agree.

Years later, when the Twin Towers were brought down to the ground, leaving a wash of ash and blood and fire, I cornered the TV as they replayed that dramatic scene over and again. By the twentieth or the fifty-first time I saw this monstrous crime unfold, well, I no longer understood the meaning of the image. And with each successive replay, the image repeating weeks, months later, the punch of the imagery was now lost even further. Even as I watched flaming bodies cartwheel out of the windows. By the hundredth time, I could've just as easily been viewing an episode of "CSI" or playing a video game and there'd be no difference. But this lack of distinction and my inability to empathize with this event was bewildering. I remember thinking about my father, and how he never made it to see those buildings crumble.

"This is America, Bernard! Look at the beauty, Bernard! Just look at that!"

It's always that pleasant tone of his voice that brings me back to our final moment together, in the hospital, when the cancer finally sucked the breath from his shrunken body, his grey eyes quiet, remote. What was a manageable case of prostate cancer eventually ate his body in less than a year. By the time this disease was finished with him, rotting his insides, dwarfing his robust frame to a mere net of bones, I no longer recognized the man who'd claimed to be my father all those years.

I can still see him now, his ashen skin expressionless as the image repeats over and again. He drifts, fighting his final gasp. From his bed, his dim eyes try to assert: *I'm proud of you, son.* But I wasn't too proud of myself then. Here I was in my late twenties living a double life, as the quick-slide into excessive partying had already begun, and it was obvious that I was no longer that boy, his co-pilot propped up in his cab, watching every moment the world had to offer. Instead, I was a disaster of a son. I had become someone else, someone with a dull headache and a dripping nose, someone who now had to watch his father disintegrate under those prying white lights.

"Thanks, Dad" was all I wanted to say during our last moment together, but nothing came, and for some reason the memory ends there. Whether I'm dreaming or daydreaming, I can't recycle anything past that point. I also don't remember if I spoke to anyone in my family about how I felt around the time of his death, which strikes me as strange today because my mother and sister have always been willing to discuss their feelings. I suppose I wasn't emotionally equipped or maybe I was just too scuffed up to talk. Though, today, I still have trouble articulating my feelings. I guess that's something else altogether.

And the more I think about this final moment with my father, the more I wish I'd held the old man's hand. Then maybe I could've offered some shared memory, like the day when I helped him catch those thieves who tried to steal from his cab. I was there watching these two con-men take money from my father's shirt pocket. I was a hero that day, or so I thought. Children are forever made to believe by adults that they are heroes of some kind. Parents want nothing more than for their kids to feel they have some noble purpose in this world, or at least that's how my parents raised me: *Do you remember when we were in the cab together, Dad, and we caught those thieves?*

10

DAVY CROCKETT & 1974

Last night, I was up late going through some old family photos. I found this one that must've been from 1974 or so because I looked to be about seven years old. The picture is creased down the middle, having that washed-out sepia look, but some vague emotion remains, a trace of what was: the disappearance of what was once "real." I'm on my father's shoulder, arms twined about his neck, wearing this Davy Crockett hat that I don't remember ever owning, and my sister is tugging at his pants. My mother is beside us, and we all have these magazine smiles, a strange shine that says everything is good, everything's okay, we're going to do this. This was well before my father got sick, before my family came to pieces.

For some reason, though, they don't look like themselves at all in this picture, or at least how I imagined them to be in 1974. I was hoping the image would restore the past more than it did. If anything I was now observing a row of strangers, and it's made me realize how futile recording anything can be. Who are these people? And is this any different from the book I'm trying to write? Even all the effort in the world can never bring back what's gone. So much of who we are is forgetting, obscuring memories, so we can move on with them. Without this ability, we'd all be walking in circles until our hearts gave out.

11

MY NEIGHBOR BILL, COONS & LONELINESS

I went outside to get the mail when I spotted my other neighbor Bill situating his sprinkler onto the grass. He just moved in this year after his wife left him. He has copper hair and a belly that's bigger than any part of his body, and when he leaned over to pick up the sprinkler, avoiding the arc of water, he sat it down on a new spot, which was perhaps a better fit. And that's when Bill saw me. At once, he abandoned his sprinkler and approached me with grave purpose, appearing more flustered than usual.

"Take a walk with me, old boy, will you. It's real important," he said. He guided me into his shed, which reeked of cats, to show off the traps he'd just purchased to "snag the little bastards."

"What little bastards?" I asked. I don't know why I entertain this guy.

"Funny one," he said, smiling. "Here, look, I've got some coyote urine here, too.

Those fuckers were needling through my cans all night." He held out a bottle like he was selling it to me. "This shit is the *real* shit. You can get it real cheap, too, online. I forget the site but it's real cheap."

"I'll look into it."

"So how many coons did you have last night?"

"I've seen some cats around. It's the cat lady's cats from down the block. They're everywhere."

"You can't tell the difference between a cat and a coon? I'm talking about the racoon, old boy."

"Nah, just cats."

"You're tugging my big dick, right?"

"No, I'm not. I'm tugging your…?"

"Then I guess you're just the lucky bitch on the block, aren't you? You're also dirty as shit. Were you playing in the mud or something?"

"I was helping Mrs. Davis with her garden," I said.

"Ha! Your friend, not mine. Hey, by the way, did you hear that the Brookshires are finally getting a divorce. Well, according to Dave, who spoke to Laura, who I don't necessarily trust, well, anyhow, Brookshire's wife opened their bedroom door to Brookshire with his pants wrapped at the floor, while he was giving it to his own daughter's college roommate!"

"I see." Bill made me uncomfortable, but he was lonely enough for anyone's pity. It was only last year his wife fled for another woman. And now all he had to look forward to was slouching at a desk at MTV studios, gawking at a computer screen all day, making sure the automation properly programs all of the network's shows. And I've often thought about myself being in similar position had Odie not been so forgiving all these years.

"And apparently this roommate is the spitting image of Jenna Jameson," he said.

"Jenna, who?"

"The porn star. Don't play the retard card on me," he said, smiling too much. "But yeah, I told you Brookshire was a lucky dick. Man, I would've tapped that ass, too. You ever see that poor bastard's wife?"

I shook my head, "No."

"Well, she's a filthy rag if you ask me."

"That all sounds crazy, man." Sometimes I say things when I don't mean them.

"It's not that crazy. Not to sound rude, but you need to get out more. How about next Saturday, actually? John and I, John from around the block John, are going to Porkies to see some titties and sit down to a few cold ones. You should come. You can't hide inside your house all the time," he said.

"You're probably right." He was right. But I wanted to devote all my free time towards my book. That mindless, debaucherous life no longer appealed to me.

"I am right. Catching a little poon every now and again is good for the soul, old boy." "Yeah, we'll see."

I've often wanted to tell Bill to stop talking altogether but I've never had the confidence. Plus, for every block in this town, there was probably another five "Bill's" and if I was going to talk to *anyone* at all, well, I guess it was going to be this "Bill"? To be honest, sometimes when I wouldn't speak to him for an extended period of time, a few days, a week, I'd get this craving to meet up with him, even if I knew I'd get stuck listening to his endless surface grumblings.

I looked up at the sky, a thin blue haze, when I thought I heard the drums again. But then they stopped at once. "Hey, do you ever hear those drums banging around the block?"

I asked.

"I don't hear anything."

"Not now, but before."

"I think you're hearing things, old boy. You're like my ex. You're always making shit up in your head," he said, laughing at himself.

"Never mind. All right I have to get going. I have some things to finish up."

"What are you working on?"

I had to work on the book, but I had no interest in telling him this. "I just have some bills to pay and some other stuff."

I put my hand my pockets and felt this card. I pulled it out. It was the Davey Crockett photo. I must have put in there last night, I thought.

"What's that in your hand?"

"It's nothing. I'll see you later Bill."

12

MISSING TEETH & MICK JAGGER

There were no other suicides that year at the Pierre, but there was plenty of grit and smut.

And by this point, my father had passed away. But anyway, I remember this one night at 4AM, we were in Mick Jagger's suite, blasting Stones songs, and at this particular bash Swedish-looking blow-up dolls were the main attraction, something I couldn't get into. The plastic tasted miserable and I could never get off using one of those damn things. Some of the others packed out the balcony with a video camera capturing God-knows-what on film, a few others were splayed out on the floor in Jagger's jeans, while Jimmy ran around the apartment hunting for his glasses, asking everyone over and again: "Have you seen my glasses? I lost my fucking glasses. I'm fucking blind. I can't lose my glasses." He could barely keep his breath. "My heart feels weird, too," he said. "It feels…it feels like there are these tiny horses inside kicking. I don't feel right." He grabbed his chest, panting, "What's happening?" Jimmy was always having some breakdown, but what was unusual was that no one had ever seen him wear glasses before. You'd think Shakespeare had penned the part for him by the way he was acting out the role of the "blind man."

Losing interest in Jimmy's theatrics, I fell into an all-night Jagger dance-off in the kitchen, where we showed off our best Jagger moves, while a few of the ladies, paid girls, friends of Hiro, wearing only underwear, dawdled on the travertine floor, banging along to the backbeat with pots and pans and spatulas and wooden spoons. A few minutes before this frisk, I'd licked all three of these women clean until one of the girls, Sadie, dug her nails into my back so deep that I had to push off her. "What the fuck is that?" I wailed.

Sadie, this bottle-blonde with a silicone body, giggled and ran across the room to put on some Stones, and that's when I stood up on the countertop and began to make a mockery of Jagger's talent:

"I can't get no satisfaction. I can't get no…satisfaction!" I sang, as I paraded about the countertop clapping to the rhythm. All of the girls, June and Star and Sadie, pounded the pots louder and faster, losing the pulse of the track. June, the brunette with dark silver lipstick, looked too happy to be alive. Then there was Star, the oldest of three, maybe midtwenties or so, this black Irish-looking girl, who liked to say things like "old boy" and "tigerlips." And all three of them hit those pots even louder. This is America, I remember thinking.

Chewing on a chicken wing, Jimmy scuttled into the room with a pair of coke-bottle old lady glasses. "Who the fuck's are those?" I asked, as I wheeled about the countertop. In the distance, I could hear someone in the other room racing their fingers along the piano. They were desperate to catch the beat.

Jimmy cried, "These are mine. They're my glasses. And this is *my* chicken, too," he said, taking another snag at the wing, grease glazing his lips. "It's not yours. Well, it's Jagger's chicken, too, but it's mine now, too." He took another bite. "And why were my glasses in the refrigerator? You people should know that they're my glasses. Not yours, you terrible, terrible people." He was falling apart. Coke gets you sometimes. It can bring you to your knees faster than a shotgun. But I just kept dancing, and before the song ended, June and Star transitioned into the main living area.

"Come on, old boy! We're going into the main room!" Star shrilled, begging me to join her.

So there was no choice but to follow along when I came upon the gang doubled-over in a giggle fit. Rocco, Javier, Philip, and Hiro were all inflated with delirium, a blind joy. I laughed along, not knowing what for. They had been charmed by one of our hired dancers, Melanie, who ran up to the crew screaming with her four front teeth missing. She was sporting my top hat, blood dropped from her mouth onto the sheets below.

"What did you do to your mouth, little Mel-bell?" Hiro asked in this affected Southern accent.

She tried to explain but more blood flooded forward. I didn't understand what was going on.

"You know you give me a big ol' heart-boner, little lady. A sparkling heart-boner."

"What the fuck happened to her teeth?" I asked, trying to sound confident, but the cocaine courage had already begun to fade.

No one responded, the laughing continued.

"Shouldn't we get a doctor?" I said. I knew they could hear the panic in my throat.

"Bernard, did you just say something? I didn't realize you were asked to speak, old boy? You see, I was just telling little Mel-bell about my big ol' heart-boner. And now *you're* asking about her teeth? I think you should apologize to her first, and once you're done with her you can say sorry to me, too," Hiro said. He smiled, unmoved, waiting for my reply.

"You look nervous, B. Don't be."

They crew laughed at me. I wanted to punch all of them in the throat. This was no longer a game. It was cruel.

Philip walked up to my face, a long look. He knew something about me that I didn't. His mouth slopped open, his face soaked with sweat, those diamond pupils rolling back and forth. "You're a silly black bitch," he laughed. "A real, real silly one. You know you should *respect* people, B. Respect, respect, respect. You know you don't talk to Hiro like that, and you don't talk to me like that either." The rest of the crew looked on, smirking, arms folded.

Philip went on, "I'm surprised growing up no one ever taught you about respect."

He coughed into the air and then reached for Melanie. He bent her over a chair, and began ramming her from behind. Blood swung from her lips, stringing all over the carpet. She laughed harder. We looked directly at each other. I wanted to vomit and couldn't stop staring. I wanted to hold her hand when I got an erection.

Hiro brought over a bottle of Cristal and began pouring it over her back and into her mouth. I grabbed my clothes, bolting out of the apartment into the hallway. I was shaking.

I threw up all over the floor, a mash of chewed raspberries. I ran for the back stairwell exit. When I reached the door, it occurred to me that I shouldn't have left the party early. No one breaks the crew rules, no excuses.

"What the fuck? What the fuck?" I said over and again. I threw on my pants, shirt, and jacket at the top of the stairs, and then soared down ten flights out onto the street when I realized I'd already called my mother.

"Ma?"

"Bernard, what's wrong?'

"Nothing's wrong, Ma."

The street bounced under the fluorescent light. Cabs glided in either direction. Shops reeled with customers as the night crowd flooded the pavement. When I crossed the road, I almost tagged the grille of a swerving SUV.

"You stupid nigger-fuck!" someone yelled from the passenger seat, as the vehicle veered around a delivery man on his bicycle, receding into the traffic ahead.

I covered my phone, shouting back, "You fucking asshole!"

When I picked up the phone my mother was talking: "Bernard? Bernard, where are you? Who's with you? Who's that in the background?"

"I'm at work, Ma. I'm at work."

"Then why are you calling me Bernard? It's 4AM."

"I know Ma. But I said I'd call you."

"What are you talking about?"

"Remember that?"

"Bernard, are you drunk? You're drunk. How are you drinking at work?"

"I'm not drunk."

"Bernard, where are you? I'm coming to get you."

"Ma, what are you talking about? I'm at work. You can't visit me at work. You're talking the crazy talk now, Ma."

"Where are you? I'm putting on clothes now. Tell me where you are."

"You can't come to work, Ma. Ma, I have to go. My boss needs me. I'll call you tomorrow. I'll call you tomorrow, okay Ma?"

"Bernard, are you okay? You're telling me the truth, right?"

"Why would anything not be okay? Ma, come on. Ma, I'll call you tomorrow, in the morning tomorrow. My boss needs me now. Okay, Hiro, I'm coming. Ma, I got to go."

My mother was going to kill me. Why would I call her this late? And why was that girl laughing with her goddamn teeth cut out of her face? And what the hell were Phillip and Hiro doing to her? And that's the last I remember of that night…

13

STARING AT NOTHING

Standing at the door, all day, there's a heap of downtime, lost time, when you feel you've gone nowhere. Like you've been standing in the same spot your entire life and you're not sure how you even got here. The streets seethe, moving at a frantic clip, every itch on your body comes to life, ticks that force you to pick apart the details of the avenue. Faces race down the avenue, images repeating themselves, as you pull together the fragments of peoples' lives, conversations that yo-yo the sidewalk. From the mundane to the miracle, you know all their stories, their dreams, their secrets, their disappointments.

"Museums are for fags, you're absolutely right. Are you still hungry?"

"If I'm not famous next year then I'm going to kill myself."

"I think the Yankees have a shot this year. This city needs a win."

"Did you hear about the man beaten to death in Central Park? Not the girl who was raped but the guy who looked like rotten meat on TV?"

I was at the Roosevelt Hotel today, holding my post, lifting luggage, working for tips, staring at nothing, again, while two men across the street were installing a brand new surveillance system.

"I'll take that suitcase, Miss." I grabbed her bag and walked her toward the taxi lingering at the curb.

"Thank you, very much," she said, not looking at me, putting a five dollar bill in my hand—just another person passing through my life.

And the rest of the day, even as I tried to distract myself with the routine of the workday, I still couldn't get that bloody girl out of my head. The flow of gore falling from her mouth, and it seems the more I loop through my old journals the less interested I've become in reading them. I almost wish I never went into that shed and read a single line in any of these notebooks. It's been so long since I've thought about all this, and why I chose to revive this story now, well, I'm not so sure. This morning, I almost couldn't kiss my daughter goodbye. I felt embarrassed to be her father. I've never felt that before.

4AM: I couldn't sleep, so I went out to my front porch. I was surrounded by the crickets, the highway, the stars, all one sound, and I thought about how my daughter could never see this book. She doesn't need to see this part of her father.

When I looked to the left, Bill was on his porch, bracing a shotgun. "Morning, old boy. You heard those damn coons, too, I gather?"

A cat climbed out of my garbage can and Bill cocked his gun. When he realized it was a cat, he put the gun to this side.

"Meow!"

"You're not going to shoot the cat are you?" I asked.

"It's a BB gun, old boy." He aimed and shot at the bush. The cat skittered across the yard. "It's not even real." He held the gun above his head. "You see what I mean? It's just a fake gun. You get too nervous too easily, old boy."

14

THE SQUIRREL-LADY & WAITING IN THE RAIN

The morning after I saw that bloody girl, I woke up to a silver pony-tailed woman feeding squirrels out of her palm. For a moment, I thought it was that same lemon-scented cocaine-freak again, but it was someone else. The tall trees above rocked easy over the shaded lawn and I had a plate of nachos on my lap. I realized I was in the middle of Forest Park, around the block from my apartment, a spot I'd hit to balance my nerves. Long thick woods, horse trails, bike paths, walkways, a rural sanctuary that no longer seemed to be Queens.

"Come here babies," the squirrel-lady sung in some made-up melody.

The lady dug into her sack of feed and showered this run of squirrels with a few handfuls. When she turned around, smiling from her sun-charred skin, I saw the puffy-pink letters on her baggy t-shirt, advertising: "YOU CAN'T BUY LOVE." I found her fascinating.

She didn't care how she was seen.

"Come here babies. Come here baby squirrels," she lulled.

I walked toward her to tell her I liked her shirt, and to ask where I could get one. I thought maybe I'd pick one up for my mother to make amends for last night's phone call.

"Hi. Excuse me? Hi. I really like your shirt. Not for me, but for my mother. Would you mind telling me where you got it from?"

She said nothing, appearing petrified. I assumed she didn't speak English.

Above the clouds gathered, racing the skyline, the trees leaned and the leaves curled.

I said, "I'm sorry to bother you. I was just wondering, well, because of my mother." She looked right through me. "You don't speak English?" She kept looking. "You don't speak at all? But weren't you just singing? Now you're just gonna stare at me?"

She turned and began singing, again, "Come here babies. Come here squirrel babies."

I gave up. My head pounded. I had to call my mother before she had the whole town out on a search-party. I went back to the bench and sat down. The first few raindrops fell, and even still I contemplated going back to sleep, not wanting to deal with anything. Across the way, I saw a gaggle of boys playing handball in the church yard. They had this selfpossession, competiveness, they radiated youth. In the distance, I heard a car backfire. The sound was so intense it sent one suit flying toward the pavement. "Get down to the ground!" he shrieked. There was a cold terror in his eyes, and when he stood up and brushed off the dirt and embarrassment, he smiled to the few of us who watched his fall and went on with his day, picking up his phone, pretending someone had called him.

The rain now shot of out the sky. I saw the squirrel-lady throw up her umbrella, whisking her way out of the park. I left too. I needed to go home. It was ten blocks away. I was going to ruin the tux, which I shouldn't have worn home in the first place. If Hiro found out I'd be dead.

When I got back to my apartment, my mother was out front waiting in her car. She saw me and turned off the lights and shot out of the driver's seat without a jacket. Running toward me, she looked like she about to break something.

"I've been calling you all day," she said. "I've called you ten times now. Why are you not answering your mother's phone calls?"

The rain wouldn't give up. She was soaked and for the first time she appeared tired, old. The beauty of my mother, fresh and light, had gathered into a web of spidery lines etched into her face.

"You called me?" I asked.

"Don't do that. You know I called you."

It was obvious to both of us that there was something wrong with the situation. I should've been the one looking out for her, and maybe by not doing anything at all, I was protecting myself from doing the "wrong thing," something I'd been avoiding my whole life.

"I'm sorry, Ma. I didn't see that you called. I didn't. I'm sorry about that." I couldn't give her my eyes.

"You weren't at work last night. I know you weren't."

I could see that she wanted to cry or yell or something but she wouldn't allow herself. And she wouldn't say what she wanted to say. She held it all in. Looking back, I now know that she not only suffered the loss of her husband, but it was even more difficult to watch her children, even if we were in our twenties, lose their father, that sense of stability. And back then my mother refused to allow time to move forward. She thought she could control it, just so Isabella and I wouldn't have to get hurt ever again.

"Tell me the truth, Bernard," she said.

"Ma, what are you talking about?" Even I couldn't convince myself.

"Bernard, where are you? Do you ever think about anyone else? You're going to end up dead somewhere."

But I couldn't hear her anymore.

She added, almost inaudibly, "What do you think Daddy would say?"

I was wet and wanted a drink. And having your mother remind you of everything you've done wrong in life is never a priority, especially when you're an adult and quite capable of choosing your own disasters.

"I hear you, Ma. But you need to get out of the rain."

"I'm not. I can't."

"Come upstairs for a minute, Ma."

"No, I can't. I have to go, Bernard."

"Then go home, Ma. You have to get out of the rain." I went for her hand, a loose grip. "You're going to get sick, Ma."

"What's wrong with my boy?" The problem was there was nothing wrong. I was an average nobody raised by a loving family. Sure, I was first-generation immigrant, and yeah my father had passed away, but my problems weren't particularly special.

She pressed a kiss on my cheek, hugging me.

"Bye, Ma." I let go, turned, and walked to my door. A shabby old man sat on the stoop, his clothes drenched, his mouth puckered, a fish sucking hard for air.

"What happened to the back of your pants?" my mother called out from her car.

"Ma, go home. I'm fine." I looked at the back of my pants. They were torn at the seam. How this happened, I'm not sure.

For an instant I felt guilty, and as soon as I got upstairs and popped a beer and hopped into a hot shower, I forgot everything.

This morning, I called my mother and reminded her of that day when we stood out in the rain together. I apologized, perhaps a little too in earnest, considering we were so many years removed.

My mother replied, "You're not remembering it right. That didn't happen. I wouldn't have stood in the rain."

"You're right, Ma. I'm probably confusing this with something else."

"It was your father who loved the rain. Not me."

According to her, my father always said it reminded him of "the magic of the movies" and of "America" and that it was "pure romance."

She said, "He'd try to bring me outside any time it was about to pour. You're lucky your mother was a lot stronger back then."

"You're still strong, Ma."

"I have many more stories about your father that I'm sure you've never heard."

"Like what?"

"Remind me before it's my time to go, to tell you *all* about it. Your father was an *interesting* man, and that's all I'm going to say."

"Can you tell me at least something right now?"

"Ha! You're just like him. You can't ever wait."

"I can wait."

"Good, we'll wait then."

"But what was he like?"

15

MADISON SICK, THE BRONX ZOO & A THOUSAND FACES

Today Madison was laid up bed with a stomach virus. All night and morning she was throwing up, never making it to school. And because Odie had an important business meeting this morning she couldn't stay home to take of care Madison. So I called in sick, too. Not only would I take care of her, I thought, but maybe there would be some time to work on the book. It's not easy to find time and space to write. Each time I think I have a good idea, or I get closer to understanding something about myself, my family, my past, it's suddenly interrupted by "life." The writing then comes out fractured, never fully realized.

Anyhow, Madison stayed upstairs all morning. From the bottom of the steps, I heard the cartoons booming from her TV.

"Do you want some Pepto-Bismol, kiddo?" I yelled up the stairs.

"No, thanks, Daddy," Madison said.

It never feels good when your child is sick. Any time they experience a shred of discomfort you seem to bear their pain. It's only after your child gets their first illness and you hear that steady whimper rip through the night that you begin to understand this inestimable parent-child bond. You'll never love anyone, anything more than your own.

I remember when Madison was just five months old and we were still living in Forest Hills, her chest had become filled with mucus. That night I stayed up until the morning, holding her against me. Standing at the window, poring over the street, I listened to each labored breath. Orange light filled the empty road below, a senseless wind slapped at the windows, rattling the street signs that lined the sidewalk, and the stoplight swayed in no particular direction. Every now and then Madison would cough, her body constricting, and I would try to calm her, rock her. It was too much listening to her wordless cries. In that moment, I realized not only had Odie and I passed the privilege of existence to this little girl, but also the inevitability of suffering, the constraints of time, and the burden of being.

Last week, I brought Madison to the Bronx Zoo. Odie had a "ton of work to catch up on." So Madison and I walked around munching on hot dogs and naming almost every animal in the place. She rode on my shoulders, steering our trip.

"Turn here, Daddy! Turn! I want to see the lions!"

"The lions!"

"Yes, yes!" I often wonder if Madison wasn't here would I be the same person. She makes life bearable.

"Okay, let's call our lion friend 'Mr. Lion Friend.'" I said.

"No, Dad, that's stupid," she laughed.

"Sweetie, you can't name him 'Stupid'? I don't think 'Mr. Lion Friend' would appreciate it if we called him 'Stupid.'"

"You know what I *mean*. Dad-dddy! Stop!"

As a kid I don't remember going to the zoo, and I wonder if that's why I brought her there, to fulfill a missing wish. Thinking about it now, I suppose my parents had every intention of bringing me there, but life probably intervened. There was one particular dinner, I recall, when I begged and wailed for them to take me. It wasn't fair, I thought, all my friends had seen this new Panda Bear exhibit.

"Come on!" I moaned.

"Bernard, we're going to church. And then I have to go food shopping. We will go to the zoo another day. I promise you." That zoo trip never came, but I'm sure my parents meant no harm.

"Come on!" I stomped my foot.

"Bernard, you're a Montpeirous, and you need to start to act like one."

I wish I could pull more from that day. But I'm sure my father went on to tell me to eat the rest of my food, and to respect my mother. "Your mother worked hard on making this meal for us," he'd often say. And she did because there was always a plateful of some Haitian cuisine waiting for us, whether it was rice and beans or chicken or pork or fried plantains or piklis. To be honest, though, I really don't recall anything else about that particular dinner. It all seems to fuse into one big family gathering, which is frustrating considering I'm attempting to write a book that intends to "remember."

Anyhow, the Haitian experience my house wasn't confined to food. We had Haitian friends, a Haitian God, Haitian ideas, and Haitian art—all things Haitian—you couldn't escape it. I even recall that oversized painting that hung in our living room, depicting my great grandfather, the President, Sylvain Salnave, in full military regalia. His imperial stare followed me everywhere I went in that old apartment, and his omnipresence had the effect of reminding me where we came from. The past was always nearby.

Once when I was six or seven, I nicked a cookie from the cabinet and hid under an ottoman in the living room. The contraband cookie was swallowed in one bite, and I nearly choked as a result. Not only was I terrified that my parents would find me out, but I also had the unnerving feeling that my great grandfather was watching my every move. At that instant, I remember thinking I was not a good "Montpeirous."

My mother found me hiding and asked me, "Bernard what are doing under there?

And what did you just eat?"

I pointed toward the wall where my great grandfather hung. "That painting scared me."

"It's okay, sweetie. But what did you eat? You know we're eating dinner soon. Did you take a cookie?"

"No, I didn't take anything. I didn't eat anything."

As an adult, I don't know if I ever became the "Montpeirous" or the "Haitian" my parents would've liked me to be. Maybe I never will. I think I've been absorbed wholly by American culture. My wife is American, my daughter, too. And these days I'm not sure if that's how I want it to be. Somehow that American shine from my youth doesn't shimmer as it once did. That burn for "more-more-more" all seems to be a cruel mistake. And yet it's so easy to forget where you came from, who you are, what you were like. It's as if we're a thousand faces in one lifetime, and our age is the only thing that defines us. To be thirteen years old has nothing to do with forty-one nor has it any relationship to sixty-five.

16

MY MOTHER & THE ZOO

I called my mother just a few minutes ago, to double-check if we ever went to the zoo.

"Did we go to the zoo when we were kids?" I asked.

"How would I know? That was a long time ago," she said. She was right about all the years that had transpired but how could we both forget something simple and seemingly memorable like this.

"Ma, can you turn the TV down in the background. It's hard for me to hear you. What are you even watching?" I heard her stand up and the TV went silent. "What were you watching?"

"The millionaire show. What's it called? The 'Who Wants the Millionaire? The millionaire show, you know.'" Her voice sounded thin, fatigued.

"Really? Since when do you…never mind. So do you remember taking us there when we were kids?"

"Why are you asking me this now?"

I had to know. I don't why I did. It's important to me, my life, regardless of how minor it may seem.

"I was wondering. Because I took Madison last week, and I don't remember going as a kid," I said.

"Now I remember. Of course, we went to the zoo. All kids go to the zoo. I remember that you and Isabella loved it."

"I don't remember it. Maybe you took her, and not me?"

"Bernard, you probably went even a few times. Now I remember, you liked that bear. I forget which one, but you liked a bear. "

We didn't go. But what's the sense in contesting your mother?

17

MY SISTER & THE ZOO

After I hung up with my mother, I called my sister.
"Did we go to the zoo when were kids?" I asked.
"I never went." Isabella said.
"Good."
"What do you mean 'good'?"
"Well, not 'good.' But I thought I was losing my shit. I just got off the phone with Mom, and she said we did go, and that I liked a bear or something."
"Yeah, that's right. Now I remember. You liked that Panda Bear. I think I remember going now. Yeah, we definitely went. I'm sure of it now."

From the kitchen, I heard my doorbell ring. Then I heard Bill's voice through the window. "You in there, old boy?" I wasn't going to answer it. "Got some good news for you."

I said, "We didn't go, Izzie. You just said we didn't. And I know we didn't."
"No, I think Mom is right on this one."
"No, she's not. I shouldn't have said Mom said that. You're probably just confusing it now after I said Mom said that." Every family memory appears to be a composite of ideas, misinformation,

reshuffled by time, over and again, meant only to appease an individual's need at that particular moment.

"Why are you obsessing over this, anyhow?"

"I'm not obsessing over this. I just wanted to know. It's for my book. I wanted to write a chapter about it."

"Wait, your book is about *not* going to the zoo? What are you even writing? I thought it was supposed to be about the hotel you used to work at? Now you are writing about zoos? Do people read books about zoos? But, hey, listen, Bernard I have to go. The man just showed up in his truck to fix the leak in my basement. But I'll call you soon. I'll call you later, actually, after I get my nails and hair done. I'm being observed by my principal and superintendent on Monday morning and I need to not look like a mess."

"Whatever's good, Izzie," I said.

"Are you being sarcastic?"

"No, I was being genuine. I was saying 'Whatever *is* good for you.'"

"Well, you're 'genuine' sounds fake. Okay, anyhow, I have to go. That nail appointment is soon. You really don't remember the Panda, huh? I think you even tried to feed him. Or I fed him."

Even if we did go to the zoo, what does it matter? I don't remember it. So it might as well be I didn't go. I need to stop fixating over this.

When I got off the phone, Odie was in the kitchen with her hand holding up her forehead.

"What's the matter?" I asked.

"You don't hear that?" she asked.

"Hear what?"

"The drums, Bernard. The drums. I can't take it anymore. It's constant. It's not music. It's madness."

"Pretend it's like the Rolling Stones or something playing in your backyard." She stared at me with disgust. "I'll go over there a little later and talk to them."

"Talk to them? I want to go over there and smash those freaking things to pieces. I can't finish a thought, anymore."

"Welcome to the suburbs," I said, smiling. She didn't laugh, and I never went around the block, because Madison needed help with her homework, and then I fell asleep watching Charlie Rose talking about the death of the public school system in this country.

18

LOST TIME, DOG MEAT & A PRIVATE SCOLDING

A few weeks after my mother stood out in the rain and reconstructed the brutal truth of my young adulthood: that I was going to be a bachelor for the remainder of my life, well, on that day I overheard some pregnant lady raving into her phone. Before her excited voice hit me, I'd been idling the afternoon away, staring at the colossal billboard across the street which depicted this rugged-looking solider with a big-angry smile and an assault rifle. The poster said in this garish yellow-green lettering: "EVEN *YOU* COULD BE A HERO!" It was hard to avoid. Sometimes I'd gawk at this billboard for hours at a time, and there'd always be a new advertisement every month, something more exciting, more incisive.

By early evening that day the hotel crowd had tapered off. Michael Jackson was the last of the lot come through. Only a few other fancy skirts flitted by, while clips of sidewalk chatter began to enter the foreground, which was when this pregnant lady paused in front of the door. She had a corkscrew bun and wore a long pale green flower-print dress.

"We can paint the room blue or light blue. What do you think will be better? Okay, I like just blue too. Yes, yes, yes. I'm scared but it's a good scared. Are you scared too?

Good. So you're scared too? But a good scared, right? Not a bad scared," she said.

She pivoted on her heel, and then once more.

"So we'll do regular blue then. Love you, too. Love you more," she added. After she hung up the phone, tears came to her eyes. She looked over at me, smiling, when she lost her balance on her heels, forcing her to topple to the concrete.

I rushed toward her. "Are you okay, Miss?"

"Yes, yes, I'm fine. Though I probably gave the little guy a bit of a ride," she said, holding her stomach as she wiped her cheeks, grinning.

"Do you need me to call a doctor?"

"No, I'm okay, thank you."

I held out my hand and helped her up. "You sure you don't want me to call a doctor?"

"No, no. I'm just happy, that's all." She wept some more, her make-up washed down her face. "I' haven't felt this way in a long time. It's a shame it's taken me twenty-five years to realize that it's okay to be happy."

"That's sounds like a long time to wait for anything." I said. But I didn't know what I meant when I said it.

"Are you happy, too?" she asked, her hands folded over her belly. No one had ever asked me that question before, and so I wasn't sure if I was. In the past, if I got high or got laid that meant it was a good night.

But before I could respond, Philip came charging outside to see why I'd left my post. His eyes were focused on the pavement. "Is everything okay here, Bernard?" he said, simulating concern.

"Yeah, Philip, we're good," I said.

"Well, okay then," Philip said, forcing a smile.

"I was just telling this gentleman that I was happy," she said.

"Well, that's very nice Miss that you feel that way," Philip said, his face tightened. "Okay, Bernard, well, Hiro just told me he wants to talk to you. So Miss, we're going to have to go. You have a nice day, now."

"Yeah, have good day," I said. I wanted to hold her hand.

"You too!" She wiped her face, again.

Philip walked ahead through the door, and through the glass beckoned me to follow.

"Good luck to you and your husband," I pointed to her belly.

"My girlfriend, you mean. I don't have a husband."

"Then good luck to you and your girlfriend."

"Stay happy," she giggled. When she said that, I realized I wasn't happy. Philip then spiraled through the glass doors, "Bernard! I said let's go now!"

"I have to go. It was nice meeting you," I said.

"You too," she said.

I didn't want to leave her. She seemed vulnerable and kind, unlike everyone else in my life at that time.

"Are you listening to me, Bernard?" Phillip asked. I didn't need to be spoken to that way, but he had my attention.

Once we were inside it was obvious Hiro didn't want to talk to me. He had left the hotel an hour before and wasn't coming back until tomorrow. Philip just didn't want me consoling the "loons" on 5th Avenue, as he'd often said.

"Where's Hiro?" I asked.

"Come with me, Bernard."

I wanted to call this bastard out on his lie, but couldn't. Ever since I ran out of that party with the bloody call girl, every thought, each gesture felt unnatural, because I felt someone was watching me at all times. Though neither boss ever confronted me about leaving the party early, it was obvious they were furious with me. And I was aware of this since the day after that party with that bloody girl, when Rocco had handed over my top hat. A cigarette dangled from his lips, when he said, "You're a certifiable cretin. You could've got us all caught. You do understand the rules, Bernard, right?"

I looked around the sidewalk to see if anyone was around. "I'm sorry, Rocco, I just didn't..." I pleaded.

"I'm flabbergasted, man. It's all a game, even an idiot like you can deduce that," he said.

"I'm sorry man. I just couldn't...she was bleeding..."

"You need to grow up my man. A game is a goddamn game." He pulled the smoke out of his mouth. "You could've fucked us over real bad, man. You're lucky Hiro is the nice guy he is. I would've shot you if I was him." He then held onto the cigarette as if he were about to flick it at my face, but he just walked away, hurrying down the road toward the subway.

"Rocco!" He kept walking. "Wait a second! Ah, fuck me!" I said, kicking the concrete.

Anyhow, after Philip pulled me away from that pregnant lady, we walked into the lobby where Sylvester Stallone rushed past us toward the exit, carrying a bouquet of sunflowers.

"Good afternoon, Mr. Stallone," I said, following his feet along the marble floor. "Gentlemen," he said, barely looking over his shoulder.

When Stallone was out of sight, Philip continued, "Stay away from the weirdoes,

Bernard. How many goddamn times do I have to tell you this?"

"Okay, but..."

"Just stop there. No more weirdoes, and that's the last word."

Then one of the newer residents, I don't remember her name, walked into the room and plopped on to the sofa. Sheathed in an elegant coyote mink with fisheye earrings, she held onto this proper-looking poodle, which she leaned over to smother with a series of sloppy kisses.

"I love you, love you. Love you, little Arthur. Yes I do," she cried. She seemed distracted, as if she were speaking to everyone in the room. Money gave these women a peculiar aura. They were different in every way. They even smelled different. The lady then looked up, puzzled, and asked us, "Can you watch my little Arthur for a moment. I forgot my pocket mirror upstairs."

"Absolutely. I will see to it at once," Philip said. Whenever he spoke to the customers he used this voice that made him sound politely urgent. I think he once told me that he watched the news any chance he got so he could practice his English.

Philip ran over to Javier, who was standing at the desk counting his fingers. He must've asked Javier to watch the dog because they both came over right away. Philip then asked me to walk down the hall with him, away from this woman. We went toward the Rotunda where the guests would gather for their daily afternoon tea. This tea room was the hotel's jewel with its domed ceiling and hand painted mural scenes that stretched from the floor up to the ceiling, depicting a detailed skyline of the mythological figures Neptune, Venus, Adam, and Eve.

We stopped just outside the entrance because there were guests inside sipping tea, speaking softly. In this reedy whisper, Philip asked me, "Do you like your job here at the Pierre Hotel?"

Before I could answer Mickey walked past us, asking, "You want to get in on the quick pick?"

"Yeah, I'm in, Mickey. Get me ten and I'll pay you back. I've got a feeling I'm going to come in big tonight," Philip said.

"You want any, Bernard?" Mickey asked.

"Sure. I'll get ten, too."

"Do you have any money?"

I pulled out ten one-dollar bills and thanked him. Mickey smiled and left, fading into the crowd.

Philip turned toward me once more. "Do you like your job here at the Pierre Hotel?" "Of course."

"You understand that we have a reputation here at the Pierre to maintain."

"Yes, I know," I said, holding back my smile, because I couldn't help but picture Philip's fake mustache, his shouts of joy, while he ran around the suites with dick slapping around.

"Oh, Philip, before I forget, how do I go about getting a pair of new pants? These are my only ones left." I grabbed my waistline, saying, "The others are too tight." If I kept the conversation loose maybe he'd forget about how angry he was with me.

"Seriously, Bernard, do you think about keeping this job? Because you're real close, B." His face went slack and cool. "Do you know how many people would steal this job from you in a heartbeat?"

"Yes, I know," I said, letting out a small nervous laugh. Though we both knew I wouldn't lose my job because I had too much information on the crew with their linen parties. And I could have all of them locked up in five minutes.

"Are you laughing? I'm not laughing, Bernard. I really hope you're not laughing." "I'm sorry. I'm not laughing." I made something up. "Well, I was. But I won't. It's just, I was just thinking of that pregnant woman crying. It's not every day you see a pregnant woman crying on the sidewalk. Right?"

"She said she was happy. Did you not hear that, too? That's beside the point. Who cares if she's crying or whatever? I don't give a shit if she's bleeding to death in the street. If they're not a customer then you don't help them. Concentrate on our clients. Do you think someone like Stallone gives half a dick if you're acting like a super hero for some freak on the street? You're a luggage laborer not a psychiatrist, Bernard. Is that understood?"

Philip's phone rang and he looked down at the caller ID. His demeanor now relaxed.

He answered his phone as if placating a child.

"Hi-iii. I know. I know. I've been working late. I know honey. I am. I am." I could hear someone reprimanding him through the phone. I wanted to laugh again and thank the person on the phone with him. "Hold on, honey. I know I made a mistake. Just a second now. Just hold on. I know. I know I should've."

Philip covered his mouthpiece, glaring at me. "I have to take this, Bernard. I hope you understood what I just went over. You're real close, B. You catch my drift there, guy? Now get back to your post."

He turned, and then spoke into the phone, using that same saccharine tone.

I guess I did understand, and ordinarily I'd try to stifle my emotions, but something about that pregnant woman's candidness, her effusive affection, made it clear that since I started working here I'd suppressed everything. I'm sure people like this woman pass by my door every day but the difference was I was now looking for someone like her to enter my life. I suddenly wanted to be that woman's lover or whoever she was gushing to. I wanted to paint my son's room blue or light blue. I wanted to be "good-scared." I was bored by the party and having no one to wake up to in the morning. Maybe my mother was right that I should find someone to even me out. Where would I go? Who would I talk to? New York was one giant deaf ear, and you could shout yourself red before anyone was moved by your pleas.

A lonely six pack of Budweiser later and I was folded into the sofa, my tongue dried to the leather, the blue glare of the TV slashing through my dreams, and any inspiration drawn from the afternoon's exchange with that pregnant lady had all but disappeared.

Start again.

19

BILL CALLS AT 7AM

I answered the phone: "Hello?"
"Who is this?" I looked at my alarm clock. It was 7AM. The blinds were shut and Odie was rubbing her eyes.
"You don't recognize my voice? C'mon old boy? It's Bill. Your bud Bill from next door, Bill?"
"Is everything okay? What time is it, man?"
"Never mind that. Listen you're never going to believe this. I have to tell you something real important."
"Bill, what time is it. It's Saturday, man."
"Listen, you know that Jenna Jameson chick I was telling you about? The college babe I was telling you about?"
"Bill, I'm too tired to understand anything right now. I'll call you back." I don't know why I can't speak up for myself. I should've kindly scolded him right then. But the insecurities of my youth, of not being able to say what I want, when I want, have permeated my adult years, too.
"No, no listen first. It's important. Remember the chick Brookshire gave it to?"
"I don't know who you're talking about."
"Well, I gave it to her, too. Last night in the diner parking lot, man. It was fireworks, old boy. I was like a young buck, again. Bam, bam, boner all night long!"

How can you call someone a liar? It seems that everyone builds up their life's small triumphs, however imaginary they may be. It gives them a shred of purpose, a reason to continue. I only know this because through the years I've recognized this quality in myself, over and again.

"Who is that?" Odie asked. "Who's calling this early?"

"Bill, I have to go back to sleep, man."

Odie said, "What's wrong with that guy?"

I hung up, and few minutes later I think I heard someone knocking at the door. Or was it the drums, again?

20

THEIVES, TAXIS, & HARSH LIGHT

This morning I woke to a panic, and Odie almost jumped out of bed, thinking something terrible had happened.

"What's wrong!" she cried.

"Nothing. Nothing's wrong."

"Then what was that! I thought you were dying."

"I'm not dying."

Lately, my dreams have been riddled by my father, something I've been hesitant to address in this book because it might slow down the progress of the linen stories. It's been the same nightmare three times this week. There I am by the old man's side in that grey dawn of that hospital light. He's dying once more. It's our last minutes together. Again, I can't speak. Ever since I started writing this memoir-thing, I seem to revisit this exact moment with the old man, over and again. Odie says I've been tossing and talking to myself almost every night.

"Maybe you should see someone, a psychologist or a sleep doctor or something," she said.

"For what?" I asked, hooking a pillow around my head.

A few mornings ago, she even asked me what I've been dreaming about. I couldn't be that honest. People's private worlds can be so enigmatic that if you told anyone what you experienced while dreaming they'd tell you to shut up. And if Odie knew any of this, she'd convince herself that I'd lost my skull and that I'd fallen off the wagon for the last time. I couldn't do that to her again. No one should have to endure even a fraction of what she's had to all these years together. Most wives would've left a long time ago. For some reason, each morning when I wake up, she's there waiting for me, honey hair and honey smile. Even after three miscarriages, and just as I stumbled right through my thirties, in and out of rehab and AA, holding on to nothing but an old habit, she was always right next to me, all those bright beginnings. If there ever was an angel, Odie was first-class.

"You were yelling last night in your sleep, again," she said. She propped herself up against two pillows; the sheet fell to her narrowing waistline, exposing her breasts.

"I don't remember that."

"That's because you were asleep."

"But I would've known if I was yelling all night long."

"Why would I lie to you, Bernard? And I never said all night long."

"Okay, so what's the problem, anyway? People talk when they sleep. Lots of people do."

"Bernard, why are you so resistant to the idea of seeing someone?"

"What time are your parents coming over today?" I got out of bed and walked toward the window. Mrs. Davis stood in the street, the scrolling dawn behind her, as she raked dirt into the sewer hole, each stroke measured, self-possessed. It was her morning ritual, a way of putting aside the present. "Bernard?"

"What? I just asked you what time your parents are coming. You didn't answer my question."

"You're an ass. Do whatever you want. You always did anyway." Odie stood up and threw a pillow at me.

But yeah, the clarity and frequency of this recurrent dream with my father reminded me of one particular conversation I had with this chatty doctor I met years ago, when I first started working the Pierre door. And it was just the other day while sifting through one of my old journals that I came upon this doctor, someone who'd I put out of mind for years, and maybe that's why I'm remembering it now.

Anyway, this doctor was thirty or so, and despite his harsh European accent, he wasn't any different than anyone else who hung by the door, whether out of loneliness or boredom or whatever. In this industry, you find out quickly that if you spend enough time on that sidewalk people will come to you to unburden themselves. I've tuned into the wildest of concessions: funerals, births, affairs, murders, and every other grievance found in this senseless city. As a doorman you get good at listening to it all or at least pretending to.

And this doctor could talk, and seemingly about nothing, as I followed the cars and people that wheeled by as he jabbered on. It was one of those crisp fall afternoons where a silver-blue sheen envelops your surroundings, when the country air overruns the city, making everything feel more than real.

"Nice day out, hey," he said, clenching a book in his hand. He had this nervous habit of whistling through his teeth whenever he wasn't speaking.

"Yes, I suppose it is," I said. "So how long are you in town for?"

"Not long. Just a week. Just getting a taste of the States. That should be enough."

"Are you going to see any of the sights while you're here?"

"Not planning on it." There were long pauses between sentences; each word was said as if it had special meaning. I wanted to talk that way, think that way. "But, I am going to see the film '*Wild* Strawberries' tonight with a dear good friend of mine."

"Wild what?"

"'Wild Strawberries.' It's an Ingmar Bergman film. You never heard of it?" He clamped his book tighter and let off a whistle. I'd never seen anyone look angry while they whistled.

"Oh, I don't keep up with the new flicks. I work too much lately, I guess." I should've told I'd seen Bergman's film ten times.

"It's a classic from the 50's. It's about an old man who recalls his childhood. It's Bergman's most optimistic. You Americans are a gas."

"A gas?"

"You're funny, that is." He looked me straight in the eye. "It's just one big party here in the States, huh?"

"Well, we like to have a good time."

"In all honesty, and don't take offense to this, but I envy your people's absenteeism. *Emptiness*, my friend, is a beautiful and enviable thing. And I say that sincerely." He looked right at me. "Though I suppose it never hurts to wake up in the morning?" He whistled, again. "Well, unless of course you've got one of those hangovers," he said, chuckling to himself.

Then about five minutes into our conversation, the momentum took an unexpected, drastic turn. It was just after I'd mentioned I hardly pay attention to my dreams.

"You never think about them?"

"No, not really. Why do you?"

Somehow this lone comment offended his entire sense of reason, so much so that he went on this intellectual tirade for at least fifteen minutes, emphasizing the importance of attending to the unconscious mind.

"Of course I do! Ha! Most people do!" he said, raising his voice.

His confidence made me feel insignificant. Here I was lugging suitcases, listening to some guy politely ridicule me because I didn't consider my dreams.

The doctor now looked at me, a long look of pity, and said, "So how do you do it?

How do you live without asking the pertinent questions?"

"I'm not sure what you're saying."

According to him, in order to understand your waking life you have to deconstruct the reality of your dreams. If I remember correctly, the expression he'd rattled off more than a few times was: "Memory begins elsewhere."

"Well, what will my dreams tell me?" I asked.

"How am I supposed to know?" He shook his head in disgust. "Do they really need to *tell you* anything? Isn't it enough just to acknowledge that they exist? I mean, you're dreams are real, old boy."

Initially, his ideas had no impact on me. It was just more eccentric banter, something that I'd grown accustomed to over the years. Yet it seems now the more I push forward with this book, and the more I try to understand my past, the more this quirky doctor's ideas resonate with me. As each time I circle back to that final moment, that same dream, when my old man finally passed, the moment appears even more real, imbued with more meaning.

It's always that same cool metal chair, those harsh lights, and his quick soft pant, as life moved away from him. I held cotton balls too, if I remember right, as I dipped them into a cup of water and pressed them to his mouth. He didn't drink any of it, his lips moistened. I'm sure I was drunk or high and I wanted to talk. I wanted to share something light and loose, something that might mitigate the pain:

> *Do you remember when we caught those thieves? The sun was a blister that day. We drove around all over the Upper East Side looking for passengers. You told me to keep an eye out for the people that looked like they had money. You told me to look at their coats and jewelry.*
>
> *You said if they look happy they have money.*

But I can never finish the story. I can't rally the courage, and I don't know why. Then my sister walks in, then my mother, slow and empty. We stand around the bed, arms around each other, and no one speaks. I can hear their tears and I won't look. I'm embarrassed. I'm not sure why. From the periphery, their faces are smears, and those damn hospital lights, that doctor whistling in-and-out of the hallways, my head burns, and when I look back at my father, I see flowers, red sunflowers, pouring from his mouth, his ears, his eye sockets, shrouding his body, the bed, spilling out onto the floor, when I wake...

...and it all comes spiraling back, the walls take shape, the TV in its proper place, the dresser, Odie's soft breath rising, falling, my daughter Madison asleep in the other room, and I'm still a NYC doorman and thank God there's no more cocaine, no more fuck-parties, no more forgetting myself.

21

THE ZOO ONE LAST TIME

"Ma, are you sure?"

"I'm sure, Bernard. I'm sure. You asked me this already?" She sounded annoyed. "I told you this already. Why are you making me repeat myself?"

"Are there any pictures? I mean, do you have any pictures from when we went?"

"I don't know. I'll have to look."

"Okay, so when you get a chance, can you look for me?"

"I just said I'll look, I said. I'll look tomorrow. Just remind me, tomorrow. You're losing it, Bernard."

"Okay, I'll remind you. I'm sure that we didn't go."

"You're just like your father."

"You keep saying that. What does that even mean?"

"It means what it means. You're just like him, that's all. And why does any of this zoo stuff matter, anyhow? That was so long ago."

"Is it a good thing that I'm like my father?"

"It's not a bad thing."

"Then why do you say it like that?"

"I don't know what you're talking about. Your father was a good man, okay. Is that what you want to hear? He was good to all of us. When am I going to see my granddaughter?"

"How about next week, Ma?"

THE REVOLVING DOOR

There was only one time when my father lost it on me, *one time*. It was after I stole his cab and crashed his into a parked car. I was fourteen. Maybe I was thirteen, and I think any other father would've hung their kid if they pulled this on them. And I know, all kids are fated to slip, ignorance and mischief—the glue of youth—but I also know most of them know when to apply restraint when demoralizing their parents.

Anyway, it was a cinch to snatch the old man's keys because each night he'd leave them out on the kitchen table, and by the time I slipped out that door, ignition key in hand, I was already down the block, foot to the floor, the windows down, a skein of lights and cars, a splatter of stars, all wheeling by the windshield. And I rode that night with my father in mind, shadowing all of his old moves from behind that wheel. And now my poor parents, I thought, were miles away and probably fast asleep, and I couldn't have been happier.

I hung my head out the window, and let my voice ring out, "New York!" Because youth is not about guilt, it's about *youth*, and *youth* is forgivable. So there I was sailing about town, veering between cars, sliding beyond stop signs and red lights, until I had to bang on the brakes, skidding, ramming the rear-end of this old Ford pickup resting at a light.

"Fuck me!" I hollered.

When I got home that night, my father was hot. I remember him bashing his fist against the wall, howling, as he clipped his own words: "What the hell? That's my car! You don't even know how! What the! You could've cost me! We'll all be living on the streets! You want to be homeless, boy?" I didn't know this man, and so I didn't think looking him in the eye would do any good. "Look here! Look at me, damnit!"

"Look at your father, Bernard!" my mother intervened.

"If you want to act like a fool then it's on your own terms! Out of my damn house!"

His voice, his eyes were sharp.

"Bernard, look at your father!" I said nothing. I cried inside, hoping he'd hit me because I think it would've hurt less.

"You're a disgrace to the Montpeirous name!" he shouted.

"I'm sorry! Just stop screaming at me! I don't want to be yelled at anymore!" My body shook, and I could feel the tears surfacing.

I'll stop here, as there's not much else to elaborate upon with this anecdote, well, besides that the old man didn't hold me in the same regard for a long time thereafter. He was more than disappointed, and there's nothing that breaks you more than letting your parents down.

After that night, I think my old man understood that part of being a parent is allowing your child to fall on their own. Though that's not to say that he wasn't there to shoulder me all throughout my floundering twenties—but after that night something was different. And yet I forgive my father for being my father. He was good to us, good to my family, as far as I know.

So I'm not sure why my mother keeps carrying on with her cryptic allusions that seem to infer otherwise. I'm sure my old man had his private troubles. Maybe he drank too much, and he wasn't always emotionally available, but he was still a good father. He was. And if I'm romanticizing the man, well, it's only because I'm as human as everyone else, creating private truths as I see fit.

22

HORSE SHIT, MY SHIT, & THE HAIL MARY

Back to the Pierre…
Every morning before work, I would knock out a hundred pushups, a hundred situps, eat a banana or an egg sandwich with a glass of orange juice, always a glass of orange juice, and then I'd say the Hail Mary out loud, even if I didn't believe in any of that Jesus junk. It's just that odd chance that "someone" might be listening, and this basic routine had always prepared me until this one day.

It was late August and muggy, that New York heat that traps and surrounds, when nothing moves, and I was tired of the street-honks, the taxi-whistling, the luggage-lifting, and those same blank faces jittering by in their bright colors.

"So long, see you tomorrow, Mr. Maxwell," I said.

"Do you need another light, Mr. Lynch?"

"I'll be here working all night, Mr. Simic, so if you need anything let me know."

"Mr. Brainard, did you remember everything this time?"

It was in and out that morning, a rotating cast of characters, pushing through those glass doors, when I was told that a man was shot in the face a few blocks away. Mickey decided on his break to take a stroll over there to check out what happened. He came back with his usual litter of lotto tickets and this big meat sandwich when he told us all about the half of a bloody head left out on the sidewalk in front of Burger King and that this psycho was still on the loose.

"You should've seen that fucking head," Mickey said.

"Was it the whole head?" Jimmy asked.

"Nah, just part of it. It looked like a movie to me. All we needed was some movie music and it would've been a movie," he said, laughing. "Don't you play the skin flute,

Jimmy?"

All morning there were sirens and a news station chopper hovered above. A pair of police officers stopped by to ask some questions and I had nothing to give.

"You didn't see anyone suspicious?" one cop asked.

"Nope, nothing," I said, nervously, even though I honestly hadn't seen anyone. Cops made me nervous those days. Coke makes you think you're always doing something wrong.

After the cops left, a crowd had gathered outside the front door, enclosing the supermodel Cindy Crawford, who'd stopped to chitchat with her fans. Her hair appeared to be sculpted from the bark of a tree, her body carved out of plastic. One young lady ran up to her, screeching, hugging her. She'd found her savior, as tears dropped from her eyes, she said, "Thank you, thank you, thank you!" I'm not sure what she was thanking her for, when a man with this hulking camera buzzed up to the scene and grabbed a few hundred photos. "Got you!" he barked. A young girl with braids looked up from her video game. Then a bus with a Mac computer advertisement rumbled by, stating, "Think Different." Everyone stopped to look and then resumed what they were doing.

But yeah, time dragged on that day, and I must've had fifteen or so conversations with myself throughout the morning, something doormen catch themselves doing more often than they'd like to admit. And work had been grating from the start because it was obvious some of my co-workers were giving me the cold shoulder after I was a no-show at the previous night's linen-party. I just wasn't interested in going after seeing that girl with her teeth torn out of her face. I needed a break. So I made up some last-minute excuse even though I'd already committed to the crew.

I told Jimmy at lunch, "I can't come tonight. I have to take my mother to a doctor's appointment early in the morning so I can't stay out late. Can you tell Hiro?"

"Sure. But Hiro's not going to be happy."

Apparently you're not to miss even one party. I think I would've been in less trouble if I mutilated their first born. They couldn't understand why I'd dip out on another classicnight when I could've had my balls sucked until the sun came up. Besides Jimmy, no one spoke to me or even glanced in my direction. I gathered from Jimmy that the previous night's bash was just as ribald, just as chaotic, when he told me he gave it to some porn star on this giant elephant leather sofa. I suppose the rest of the crew's reticence was part of this childish punishment, a way to make me feel even worse about myself than I already did, which only highlighted how artificial their initial affection was.

Finally, at lunch break I was able to speak with Hiro and Philip about skipping the party.

"I'm sorry I wasn't there last night. I'll be at the next one, I promise," I said.

They smiled and said nothing.

I followed with, "Was it a good time at least?"

Hiro replied, "When does your break end? Shouldn't you be back at the door by now?"

I looked at my watch, "I have another five minutes, Hiro. So, wait, was it a good time?"

"I'd get a jump on it then, amigo. You're eating into my clock," he said.

At that moment, I felt like I was looking at someone else. This was the guy who held his penis as a hammer so he could club people over the head if they didn't heed to his sexual advances, but also the same person who hid behind his tears, fixed in the middle of Madison Avenue before that suicide victim. I didn't know any of these people.

"Wait, I'm confused, when does your break end?" Hiro asked once more, his face darkened.

I could sense myself drifting from this man, from this scene that he'd created. I looked at him for what seemed like a long time. There was a profound unhappiness about him. He and his crew would always be waiting, hoping, for something better, expecting something more sensational. For this reason, I pitied him and everyone else, including myself. And that moment, I knew I had made a mistake by even associating with any of these people.

"Bernard, what the hell are you staring at?" Hiro asked. "Did you hear me? Get your big black ass back at your post before I fire it."

An hour or two after my lunch break my day really came apart. It was then I had the privilege of chasing some homeless man from the sidewalk who was conducting a private sermon with the sky, his hands treading the air above, piss all over his pants. "Jesus will eat all of you!" he repeated. "You people all hate yourselves. Jesus died for you lazy fools. You don't know what suffering is!" He spoke in fragments, making it almost impossible to understand. But he walked right up to me, tilting his head, probing my face. "Are you a good American, sir? Will you burn at the stake for your country?"

I had seen this guy before, staggering along the pavement, meddling through the bags across the street. I often imagined what his family was like. What he was like when he was a boy. He once had a father and mother at one point, too. Still, this guy had to get off our property before the guests started to complain and the tips disappeared, because New York's elite wants nothing to do with trash like this. They're the disposables of our planet, meant to skulk in the shadows, far away from the "real" people, the "real" problems of the "real" world. But I couldn't be that harsh, even during those my shallow, younger days. I'm sure this man had no family, no friends, and no past. His life was probably a bitter mix of memories and dead recollections.

"Find the forgiveness in your heart!" he bellowed. "And let Jesus into your life!

Devil, come out of this man!" His voice shook his body, his eyes deepened.

Poor bastard or not, this was preposterous, and I was going to lose all my tips and maybe even my job. I didn't care that Philip and Hiro told me never to leave my post.

Walking away from the door, I said, "Hey, you're going to have to leave the premises." There were plenty of other hotels he could show off his kitchen-sink parlor tricks to.

But he pushed right up to my face, emerging from his lice-ridden beard, a scattered stare, and whispered, "Jesus will eat you!"

"Okay, okay. I understand. Jesus will eat me. Now please just go, my man. Here, take a dollar." I reached in my pocket and pulled out a ten-dollar bill. "Here, take ten dollars, just get off my sidewalk, man."

He took the ten dollars and ripped it down the middle. It's only after you position yourself on the sidewalk for eight hours a day, and three hundred days a year, that you begin to notice the brilliance of my job: the noise and nonsense that clogs these city streets, all put on full theatrical display for anyone to see.

"Jesus died for your country and your sins. You need to *burn* at the stake old boy, burn, burn, burn old boy. American is a dying, wicked country! American is dead. You corporate whores ransacked your own goddamn land! And Jesus is gonna eat your brains out for that! But we shall all be redeemed! Yes, we shall be released! We shall be released from the darkness within!" he barked.

The more I listened to this man, the more he made sense to me. Maybe it was the way he said it, his convincing tone, and how he kept repeating what he said. "I hope he does, sir," I said. "Now you're going to have to move or I'm going to call the cops," I said.

"Jesus eats cops too. And he eats nigger boys just like you," he boomed, and then spit in my face and missed.

"What the hell is wrong you!" I should've smacked him in the teeth. I don't know what stopped me.

This man now stood up straight and his face softened, and all the tension in his forehead was released. He looked like a different person. "What's wrong with me, sir?" he asked. His voice now sounded clear and warm, calling forth the easiness of my father's voice.

I just looked at him. He smiled and almost whispered, "You know, I see you out here every day, standing there, smiling, and collecting *your* fancy tips. I see you, as I plow through my cans every day. That's right. And I'm watching you! And you all think you're virtuous because of your money? Ha! You're just lucky, that's all. But I'm just as lucky, too." He stopped for speaking, like he'd remembered something, and then continued. "Hey, you know what, why don't you ask me why I'm lucky? Ask me what I ate today? Go ahead, ask me," he said, his eyes rounding.

I said nothing.

"You're not going to guess? Well, then I'm going to tell you. I ate some leftover pizza crust that I'm sure some drunk-ass fool just couldn't finish. And it was fucking de-licious. But wait, so you're asking *me* what's *wrong* with *me*? Friend, you're not even real. You're all one big show. You're like everyone else in this damn deluded country!" He stomped his foot on the ground. "This damn dying country, I tell you! We live in a dying world, old boy!"

There were rocks in my stomach, and what he said somehow made sense.

"You're going to have to leave now," I said. My voice felt removed, somewhere else.

"I'm not going anywhere." He looked at me for what seemed a long time, and then spit in my face, as it dribbled to my nose, rolling into my lip. I should've done something but I just stood there. But I saw myself in this man, and thought about how easily anyone could fall from grace.

He added, "Maybe, friend, you should've been the one who jumped from your building." He looked the high up at the building behind me. "I think it would've saved you a whole life's worth of wasted time."

I then heard a bang down the block. I quickly turned to see if another jumper fell. It was just a truck opening its hatch to drop off some goods. I wiped my face and just left. I don't know why I didn't hit this guy.

Of course, once I turned my back, he was already weaving down the avenue toward the end of the block, creating just as furious a din with the heavens above.

After that episode, I was finished. I went to Hiro's office to tell him I had to go home, I was sick. When I went into his office he had his feet propped on the desk, sifting through the web. He immediately closed out his internet page and rose from his chair, but not before I caught a couple of sweaty Latina boobs rocking back and forth, her face bearing a look of torment.

I knocked on his door, "Excuse me, Hiro?"

He sat back down and set his eyes on the screen, again, a vague look. "Yes, Bernard."

"Is it okay if I leave early today? I'm not feeling well. It's my stomach." It was the first time I'd asked to leave work early.

"You can't make it through the next half hour?" he asked, speaking to the screen.

"I don't think so. It's hurting bad."

"You can't wait, man?"

"It's actually really bad, to be honest. I'm going to shit myself if I don't go now."

"Okay, just go. You're making me ill just looking at you."

Normally, I'd hop on the R train, but it felt good to leave work early. I decided to treat myself to a cab ride home. There was no luck catching one, so I kept walking along a crowded Madison Avenue. On every block: advertisements, storefronts, the whole world for sale, signs and billboards and posters and words and more words, attacking the senses, when the city started to slow down and show itself just enough that you could absorb its meaning, its beauty: the towering architecture, the flickering light, the people the pigeons along the sidewalks, the whiff of toasted peanuts, the sparkle, the haze along the avenue, the horse drawn carriage ride, the roan-colored breast, the forearm down to the hoof, clickclack over and again, followed by this drawn-out nicker that rose above the surrounding brabble.

I finally hailed a cab and just as I was about to open the door I stepped into a pile of horseshit. "Fucking shit!" I cried out. I think everyone within ten blocks heard me. I tried wiping it off on the side of the curb. The cabdriver didn't see anything, so I got into the backseat.

As soon as we passed over the bridge, the stench had overtaken the cab, and so this Indian–looking jerk, whose eyeballs floated in the rearview mirror, decided to drop me off a few blocks from my apartment, racing away without asking for a dime.

I had to walk the rest of the way, scraping the mess off my shoe, as the neighbors and streetwalkers gawked in mock-horror.

"Screw you," I wanted to say.

When I got to my apartment I left my shoes at the curb and went upstairs to take a shower. Five minutes and I was out the door in a pair of shorts and running shoes, ready for a jog through Flushing Meadows Park, which was just over the bridge from my Forest Hills apartment.

23

TOOTHPICKS, WHISTLING, & DAD'S DYING

That hospital dream, or whatever you'd call it, happened again; it repeats over and again, always that same moment, always a slight variation of what came before. I have to write these dreams down. They feel more vibrant than my real life, and seem to be just as important to this story as anything else. However, if this material seems irrelevant or tedious then I encourage you to skip to the next chapter and continue on with the "facts" of the story.

So there I was again, under that crude white light. I held a cotton swab up to the old man's face, and I was high and wanted to talk, to ease his ache, and perhaps my own:

> *Remember when we caught those thieves? At that point you'd let me get out of the cab and walk around the streets. I could see you beside your car looking over at me, you and that toothpick in your mouth...*

I wanted to cry but nothing...

> *...that damn toothpick that hung from your lips every day. Remember when we caught those thieves? They tried to rob*

> us blind. I caught them Dad. Do you remember? You were proud of me that day.

My father didn't respond from behind his respirator. I had no more to give. I turned around to get my jacket, when that suicide jumper from the Pierre appeared at the entrance, wearing a loud orange jumpsuit, bearing a sunny bouquet of flowers. As soon as he entered, he sat down on my father's bed and began confiding in the old man: "Daddy-man, you've seen the cocaine before, right? This is America! No problems, right sir? See you at the zoo, fat man!" the jumper said in a voice that was reminiscent of my father's.

When my father didn't react, the jumper shook his leg in a way that seemed painful.

But I couldn't confront him. I didn't want to strike up a scene.

The jumper stood up and smiled at me. He then took out his penis from his pants and began urinating on the floor. He turned to my father and tears coated his cheeks, and said, "Hey, Daddy-man, get the hell off my concrete. You going to spook the customers, you assman! Get off of here or I call the motherfucker police on you." Now he was stealing my voice. It was obvious he was trying to insult me.

I couldn't believe it. I called out for a nurse, a doctor, anyone to get this psychopath out of here. Those damn hospital lights, that goddamn doctor whistling his way through the rooms, when that pregnant lady, the happy one on the sidewalk, walked in wearing a nurse's uniform. She had a towel tucked under her arm, her mouth dropped blood, and she was missing a few teeth. My sister Isabella walked in carrying a Panda Bear, followed by my mother, who looked tired and worn from within.   Isabella put the bear on the floor and walked toward the nurse, who appeared terrified by her presence.

"Please, stay away from me. Don't do it. Please, don't hit me," the nurse begged.

Cocking back her leg, my sister kicked this nurse in the shin, over and again, she kept kicking and kicking until the woman fell to the floor bawling.

"Why would you do that to me again?" this nursed cried, grabbing at her leg. "Why would you kick me? Why would you hurt me?"

I stood and stared. The Panda was now playing with its claws. The nurse smiled and started drying the mess on the floor with her towel. The jumper shook out the rest of his piss on her back, zipped up, and ran toward the window, pressing his face to the glass.

He jumped up onto the sill and turned toward us, a spill of blood chased down his neck:

"Okay, Bernard, I'm going to do it. Here goes, I'm going to do it. Are you going to stop me? You should stop me, Bernard. You should stop me," he said, cackling, and then lifted the window and toppled out into the sky. My father stood up on the bed, his eyes shut, and began clapping. My mother, my sister and I stood arm-in-arm around the bed. They sobbed and I wouldn't look up, when I woke...

...and everything came spiraling back, the walls took shape, start again.

That was yesterday morning. Today I woke up in the middle of the night trapped in that same hospital bed, my father hovering over me, yelling: "I caught those thieves, damnit. Not you, boy! Not you. Don't lie to the people. You're not the hero, you're a pussy. Pussyboy." The old man stopped screaming and then promenaded toward the corner of the room where he grabbed Mrs. Davis from behind and lifted her flower-print dress up over her head. She had a poodle in her hands and each time my father thrust his body into hers, it was the pup that yelped with agonizing pleasure:

"This is what you wanted, right? Right?" he kept saying to no one.

Now Hiro walked in with the suicide jumper riding piggyback. The jumper dropped off and dove through the glass, while Hiro went up to my father and whispered something into his ear. My father at once gave up, pulled up his pants, and at the same time congratulated and apologized to Hiro, and then went back to bed where he fell asleep. Mrs.

Davis and Hiro walked out of the room in silence, hand-in-hand, never looking back. Through the door, my mother ran in and asked, "I thought I heard your father. Was that your father talking, again? He was talking to you, right?"

I'm not afraid, every father dies, even I'll be a dead father one day too. Just say something, will you, damnit.

24

BAKED CLAMS & A JOG IN THE PARK

I went for that jog after work, after I told Hiro I was sick. The August sun can be hell and with the constant drone of Queens' traffic it makes sense that people escape for the quiet beauty of Flushing Meadows Park. The people shuttle in from all across town to unwind here: the attractive greens, the soft blue skies, bounded by stretches of tall trees and park benches scattered throughout. It's not unusual here to see a Frisbee flown through the air or children chasing each other in circles as some health-nut peddles their bike past a wave of fashionistas spread out on a blanket sopping up the sun. They're all here to celebrate life, the good life, and if your head is fixed on right it's not too hard to embrace this.

Usually, I'd run around the lake a few times, to clear my head, and for no particular reason that afternoon, I cut through that grassy field, rerouting my typical trek. And if someone had told me that I was going to stumble upon my wife that day, sunbathing in some skin-tight shorts on this very lawn, I would've just laughed.

But there she sat, sprawled out on a blanket next to a ten speed bicycle. With her honey-brown skin and her long chestnut hair draped over a pair of headphones, I could hear the Police song "Roxanne" blaring out of her headset. And I don't know why I sat beside her. A young man's bravado, I guess. Or maybe I was just desperate for a companion.

When I first said "hello" she gave nothing back. I tried once more, "Hi, I'm Bernard." She just stared into the trees ahead.

I was dry of ideas, so I decided to play the goof, a recurring act my father performed throughout my childhood. The old man had the ability to deconstruct the most melancholic of moments. Whether I got cut from a sports team or some girl bludgeoned my heart, he would contrive this same kooky face by pressing his lips forward, crinkling his forehead, and flaring his eyes. He had a way of reminding you that life didn't have to be so serious all the time.

Craning my head a foot within her gaze, I screwed up my face, waiting for her reaction. From her vantage point, I probably looked like some cartoon-camel. She threw off her headphones, reeling back, cackling to the ground.

"Shit!" she yelped. "You're so crazy!"

"I guess I should say thanks," I said, smiling.

"What the hell was that?"

Within minutes, I'd convinced her to take a walk. I walked her bike alongside us, as we circled the park for at least an hour, speaking with the curiosity and enthusiasm of two teenagers. First it was the unpredictable August weather, and then it was about her crammed apartment in Corona, Queens, which evolved into a full-on gripe about having to grow up one day and take on adult responsibilities like laundry and making dinner.

"What are you reading?" I asked, pointing to the book in her hand.

"It's something for school."

"Something for school?"

"It's about how the sun's dying, and how all of this," she said, waving her hand in a semi-circle, "all of *this* will end one day. It's really amazing if you think about it." For a nineteen-year-old, she was more curious than anyone I'd ever met.

"I've heard this before. But we'll be long gone before the sun dies out. Though I guess you could say we're all dying, all the time, anyway."

She looked me, and I looked away, and conversation halted for a moment, as I now imagined my father's face, a long brown smile. And across the lawn, a boy held an ice cream cone as he threw a whiffle ball to his older brother, the wind working the leaves ahead. Traffic circled the distance, a bland murmur.

"Is this where you usually study?" I asked, trying to think of something besides the old man.

"It's easier to study here than at home or school." A year or so later she would tell me why she left her house that day, how her father came home in a drunken fit, picking a fight with everyone in reach.

"Where's school?" I asked.

"Columbia. Why are you walking faster?" she asked.

"Sorry, I didn't realize. I'll slow down."

It was only a matter of time before I'd boast to her about all the celebrities I met at the Pierre. Once I did, her big brown eyes blew wide open. She had-to-know every famous person I'd encountered.

"Do you get nervous being around them? I would. I think I'd be nervous especially around Madonna," she said.

"Nah, they're friends of mine. It's no big deal." The fact that I was manipulating the truth didn't matter to me then. I wanted this girl to like me, and I would do anything to make that happen.

"Well, it sounds wonderful to me. Do you know how many people would want to meet Michael Jackson or Madonna?"

She was young and easily impressed. But there was something unusual about her.

She was intuitive, present.

"What other crazy stuff has happened at your hotel?" she asked.

"Well, I don't know. Let me think. Well, not to sound too macabre but some guy a few months ago jumped out of our building and died on impact. It was insane. There were police, an ambulance, people screaming; it was a madhouse."

"Oh, my God. That's horrible. Were you there?"

"Yeah, I was. It was awful." I looked straight ahead, watching a man jog with ease, when I saw that suicide jumper's startled expression, which shaped into my father's face.

The old man would show up in my thoughts whenever he wanted to.

"What happened?" she asked. I didn't answer. Fire engines blared beyond the trees.

"Bernard? Why'd the guy jump?"

"Oh, I'm not sure to be honest. I think his wife left him. I don't know. Maybe he lost his job? That's what I was told."

She looked at me. "I'm sorry that you had to see something like that."

Everything I said she listened to. I wanted to call my mother to tell her I'd met someone. It would've made her happy. Something she hadn't felt since the day my father died. There comes a time in your life when all you want to do is make sure your mother isn't suffering anymore. I only wish I had known this earlier. I assume that's part of waking up: having to look back on all the selfish jabs you've made along the way. To be young is the most dangerous thing you'll do in this life, and I'm sure my mother's heart today, as a result, is as sore as the feet she's been walking on for the past sixty years.

"Can you make that ridiculous face again?" Odie asked.

I laughed, "I can't do it again. That's like asking a chef to bake a cake twice. Once it's out of the oven you can't put it back in."

"What are you talking about? Can you be any more abstract?" she laughed. This was the first girl that liked what I had to say. I suddenly wanted to talk, and I wasn't high.

"Do you mind if I take your bike home for you? I'll put it in my Mercedes, and then you can drive home with a complete stranger, and then later I'll come by and maybe you could even have dinner with this same person? And perhaps you'll eat seafood with him too. Because I think this guy knows this great place that makes the best baked clams in all of New York." What was I saying? This wasn't me. This outward composure denied how uneasy I felt.

"I've never had baked clams before."

"You never had baked clams! That's like saying you've never heard of the Beatles! Now I'm not so sure I can trust you," I said as I lifted her bike onto my shoulder as we walked out of the park, toward the overpass where my car was waiting in the lot on the other side. It felt odd to feel good.

I drove her home, and people flashed the streets of Corona. The crowds dotted the pavement, hurrying. There was nothing graceful about their walking. Stretching down the roadway, there were churches near Laundromats, alongside pawn shops and car washes. I caught a liquor store and a bodega on every corner, and a sidewalk of vendors leading up to those residential brick-face apartments.

When we pulled up to her place, I looked her in the eye. "Seven sound okay?" "See you soon, stranger," she said, smiling.

When I got back to my apartment I called my mother right away to let her in on the good news.

"Bernard, I'm so happy for you," she said.

"Ma, she seems smart and nice, too. And her family seems like a good family.

They're Cuban too."

"Your father would be happy for you."

After we said goodbye, she asked me to call her again before I left for the "big date" so she could wish me luck once more. The great gift of parents, I suppose, is that they're able to conceal the past no matter how bleak or disappointing it's been. If a child is happy then a parent is happy, and sometimes life can be just that simple. With this basic motherly encouragement all that came before appeared as mere preparation for this one moment going forward. She knew I'd met someone special, and she believed me when I told her Odie was the first person I could speak to without reservation.

It wasn't until years later, after Odie and I married and we had Madison, that I told her about the gritty details of the orgies and the cocaine and whatever else. She always knew something was amiss but she wasn't aware of everything or what she did know she chose to repress. I guess I opted to not tell her everything because the timing never fit. I guess I couldn't let her into my life fully. Though, some years later, even after I told her mostly everything—it was this one drunken night, after a friend's wedding—well, I'm not sure she understood much of what I said.

That evening we'd pulled up to our place and I unloaded on her. I was so inebriated that I could've told my story to the wall. I just needed to tell someone, when I said: "I was bad. You don't know. You don't even know me, Odie. You don't."

"Bernard, what are you talking about? Let's go inside."

"I used to do bad things. At these parties that I went to all the time. These fuck orgies, you know. No one knew about them. In the hotel rooms we'd just fuck all the time.

The people weren't there when we did this."

"Okay. I'm confused. So are you trying to hurt me right now?"

"No, no, no, no. I'm not going to hurt you anymore. I can't hurt you. I've got nothing on me. Here, check my pockets. Here, check. Look, no guns. No knives or anything. Here, check." I smiled and pulled out my pockets. "I got nothing. Look, here. Are you looking?" I joked. Thinking about this now, this humor eludes me.

"What are you even talking about? I'm going inside. You can stay in the car all night if you want."

"No, Odie, I'm going inside. You stay in the car if that's what *you* want to do."

We went inside and that night I told her every detail I could conjure up from those raucous days at the Pierre.

"This is who I am. I'm me," I shouted. "This is me! I'm me!"

I was ranting around the living room. I had vital information, I thought. She sat on the couch, folded against the armrest, without saying a word. Her face went limp, hazy. She had lost control of her expression. I remember thinking: I no longer have to carry this load alone. In telling her all of this, though, it was the first time I began to feel the weight of what we actually did in those days. Before that, that part of my life was never properly measured. It was just something I did as a young man, romantic and innocuous, confined to a barroom yarn over a row of drinks. When I saw a veil of tears form at Odie's eyes, I realized that perhaps I'd gone beyond being honest; it was malicious, self-serving. And as time moves forward, I'm not sure she understands today much more of what I said that evening, and for that matter, I'm not sure I do either.

25

PORNO, HOT COFFEE, & THE PRESIDENT

Saturday afternoon. Bill called me over for coffee, which usually means he wants to chat about his ex-wife or how bad his life is. And I always listen, because listening to him is a reprieve from my own problems.

"After the news is over," I said. I was interested in hearing the president's plan to bring the troops home by next month.

"That's fine. News doesn't last that long, old boy. It'll be over in two minutes. And why do you watch that bologna anyway? Everyone knows more than half of it is made up. It's make-believe. You're listening to misinformation most times, old boy. And if half of it is not true, then *none* of it is true."

"Bill, I'll be over soon."

"Just hurry your big black ass on over here. I've got some *real* big news on this side of the fence." Listening to Bill was no different than watching the news, as there was always some breaking, sensationalistic story.

"I'll be over soon."

I then turned up the TV and listened to the president detail his exit plan, elaborating his strategy a few different ways. It was strange because it seemed to me that his speech was nearly identical to the one he gave last week. Maybe he changed a few words? He then interrupted himself, denying that we were even in a war, whereby

THE REVOLVING DOOR

he reiterated: "The troops will be home soon! The war is over! The troops will be home soon. America's heroes are coming home!"

The crowd gathered was riotous, hammering their fists at the sky, and I turned off the TV. I was now more confused about things than I was before I heard him speak.

When I knocked at Bill's front door he told me to come in. He was leaned into his computer screen as if he were under a spell. There was a leftover meat sandwich and two liter bottle of Pepsi on the dining room table. All the lights in the house were off and a TV was playing somewhere in another room. It was obvious neither coffee nor his ex-wife was the reason for this invitation.

"You've *got* to see this, old boy. You've got to see this! It's the holy grail of vaginas!" He wanted to show me some new porno film he found on the web, which involved a woman placing a live snake up her vagina.

"Wild fucking shit, right? My ex-wife would've never done this," he said, smiling too much.

"Most wives wouldn't, Bill."

The lady on the screen sounded like a starved ape.

"I just can't believe it," he said.

I pretended I couldn't watch. "It's awful. You can't watch this stuff. Is that why you brought me over here, man?" The truth was it didn't affect me. I'd seen much worse, a thousand times over. I wasn't going to let him know that because the past is the past. In this world, this town, I was someone else, someone who made every effort to blend in.

"I know it's a bit gnarly but this is the *real* shit. This is the shit that happens all the time." Bill replied, turning up the volume. "You can't censor yourself and live in a bubble, old boy. You've got to see it all, if you actually want to say you were alive. I mean, people can do whatever the fuck they want, right? If we can drop bombs on countries, for example Hiroshima, Japan, and everyone can forget, then this lady getting a snake pushed up her is like a little wind in the eye, old boy."

"Well, then I guess it just doesn't interest me."

"I don't care if it interests you. What I want to know is if you think it's real? It looks real to you, right? I think it does at least. It has to be real. Who would put that much effort into making something fake?"

"I guess. I don't know. It's still gross."

"What's wrong with you? And why do you always look so friggin' tired these days?

You need to get some more sleep."

"Maybe I do."

When the snake video ended the woman curled into the mattress, her body reminded me of a burning match.

"Did you like that shit?" he asked.

"Like what?"

"Are you tugging my big dick again, old boy?" he smiled. "The damn snake bit I just showed you!"

I don't know what I felt. But I said, "I'm going home."

"Ah, don't be such a pussy." I went for the door. "Hey, wait, I wanted to ask you something. Do you think I should paint this room blue or light blue?"

"Goodbye, Bill." I opened the door. I felt myself getting closer to this guy, and the closer I got the more alone I felt, and I didn't want to feel that way.

"I caught another raccoon last night. Three in the last month. Fucker had fangs, I tell you. I'm not lying, old boy! I'm not lying to you! Why would I ever lie?"

Outside the sun was exploding behind a stretch of houses. Two boys pedaled by on their bikes, their fey cries dimming as the night sky fell.

26

ITALIAN ICES, TIGHT SHORTS, & SNAKES

There was no cocaine on that first date with Odie, and I'm not sure why. For a minute it felt right to be sober. When I turned on the car, I began to regret this. It would've pushed the night along, and she wouldn't have suspected anything. She was just under twenty years old and when I was high I was a good time. The guys at the Pierre had always said the same. And my old man always said: "The first impression is the only impression." This was coming from a man who'd spent his entire life with his knees buckled behind a taxi, making a quiet living off that first moment. So, I decided to dive headlong into the evening, a clean head, hoping we'd connect without all the fuss, without any of the nosebleeds.

The summer wind was bright and lazy, and I had the top down on the convertible, when I realized I'd forgotten to call my mother. She was probably home alone, gathered by the phone with her novel turned to that same page for the past hour, that identical passage repeating over and again, and to think she only wanted to wish me luck on my big night out. I told myself I'd ring her from the restaurant as soon we got there. If I didn't she'd probably be at my doorstep, again, waiting in whatever weather to remind me of how selfish I'd been.

When I drove up to Odie's home, it seemed the whole town was outside. And within five seconds, Odie's two little sisters, Nick and

Jojo, who I'd heard all about during our walk in the park, dropped their bicycles, racing up to me before I could get out of the car.

"Hi, you must be…" I asked the girls when I was interrupted.

"Are you famous?" the one with the tight braids and the Kool-Aid smile peeped.

"Am I famous? Well, I work at a famous hotel with famous people in it. Does that make me famous? Are you two Odie's sisters?"

"I'm Nick. That's JoJo. Is that your big white car?" Nick begged for an answer.

"Yep, it is," I said.

"Can we drive in it?" they both asked.

"I think we can do something like that. Is Odie home?"

"Are you going to marry Odie?" Jojo asked.

"You're both mini-comedians, huh? Is your big sister around?"

When Odie came out of the house in her skin-tight green dress, strutting with the confidence of a woman twice her age, I wanted to cancel our dinner plans and bring her back to my pad so we could go at it right then.

"You look amazing," I told Odie.

"That's very sweet," she said.

But then I thought I'd take her two sisters for a spin in the Mercedes for some Italian ices. All kids are enthusiasts when it comes to bright colored ices, and if Odie saw that I could be generous and that I was good with them, well, maybe she'd like me.

I said, "I was just thinking…should we take your sisters for a spin in the car to get some Italian ices before we get dinner?"

Odie smiled and her sisters sang, "We're going to get ices!"

It was only minutes before the four of us were riding through town with the top down, the air was pink as the sun set behind the low-rise buildings, and I could tell that Odie was overwhelmed. She looked back at Jojo and Nick and then smiled. I'd only met this woman six hours before but I already liked her. It's strange because even though she seemed thrilled to be out with me, I still felt unsure around her.

I was now sorry for not taking that line or two before I left, which reminded me that I had to call my mother.

We pulled up to an Italian ice shop and the kids hopped out and ran toward the window. Odie and I caught up and we all ordered cherry ices. I didn't like the flavor but I didn't want to stand out.

When I paid the clerk for the ices, Odie looked me right in the eye. She then turned to the kids and said, "Say thank you to Bernard for the ices."

They said, "Thank you!" and began licking their ices.

"No, thank *you*, for coming with me," I said. I turned back to the cashier and put a five dollar bill in the tip jar, making sure Odie saw the gesture.

But it just felt strange be part of their world. They were too nice. I was used to feeling nothing at all. To be happy only hurt, and when I saw their expressions, a child's delight, untouched, it made me want to start again, to start a new life.

Jojo asked, "Mr. Bernard, do you live in a mansion?" Her mouth was crayon red.

"Well, it's not a mansion exactly. More like an apartment, a really big apartment." I couldn't make up any stories with Odie standing right there.

"Can we drive in your car tomorrow, too?" Jojo asked.

"Sure, just ask you big sister Odie if she's okay with that."

"Can I get another ice, Mr. Bernard? Jojo's ice was bigger than mine," Nick said.

"Nickie, don't be rude," Odie said.

"That's okay. Mr. Bernard doesn't mind," I said.

"One ice is enough Nick," Odie said.

"But Odie, Jojo had more. Not fair. Well, then can I at least drive in the front seat on the way home? Please?" Nick said.

"Sure," I said.

"But that's not fair to Jojo," Odie said.

The girls walked down the block to a pet store and pressed their faces against the window.

Jojo cried, "Odie, Odie, come here, come here, look there's snakes in there. Look, snakes! Look at the snakes! Odie, come quick! Odie, can they break out of the glass?"

Nick dropped her ice and ran back toward Odie, nestling her head into Odie's dress.

Odie replied, "No, no. They're not going anywhere, Nickie." And Nick wouldn't turn around. Her hands were strapped right around Odie's thighs. I walked up to the window and tapped the glass but this one long yellow-spotted snake just hung from a branch, unmoved.

"He looks like he's been out all night," I said to Jojo, laughing at my own joke. Odie looked at me, narrowing her eyes. But if I said what I wanted to say in that moment, she would've left right there. The truth was when I saw this snake I pictured this woman Rhonda who I met at my second or third linen party. And the reason why I remember her name was because she liked to say it to herself every time someone gave it to her. "Rhonda, oh, Rhonda, oh, Rhonda!" she'd yelled. Everyone thought she was fantastic because the instant she arrived she pulled a six foot pet snake out of her duffle bag and wrapped it around her body, and then jumped on Rocco, riding him on this full-sized polar bear rug.

"Oh, Rhonda, oh Rhonda!" she cried, again.

The snake fell off a few times but Hiro and I just helped put it back on. I was so cranked that night, I could've stuck my head in that snake's mouth and it wouldn't have mattered. And we snapped so many pictures all night because it all felt so damn special and new. But I can't disclose whose suite we were in on that particular evening, because I don't think the family would be pleased. Especially if they knew Hiro convinced Rhonda to work the tail of her snake right up her vagina.

The problem was I couldn't forget the things that I wanted to forget. The imagery was everywhere, even as I looked over at Jojo, slurping up her bright ice. We don't say what we think, *ever*. I mean, could you imagine if I told Odie: "You should've seen that women's face when they finally got that snake up inside of her. But don't worry, we got pictures to prove it!"

I tapped the glass once more, when the snake looked toward me and shot its mouth wide open, fangs banging into the glass.

"What the!" I jumped back. "You motherfu…" But I caught myself.

On the car ride home, Nick and Jojo persisted with their questions until we reached Odie's house where her parents sat in the yard waiting for us. They were on folding chairs, holding hands, listening to a handheld AM radio. They were the poster family for the "good life." After my father passed away, I couldn't help but be envious of what everyone else had.

Odie said, "Mom and Dad, this is Bernard. Bernard, these are my parents." You could tell that she was nervous. She thought her family was too "poor" for me. I wish now I was kinder then. I should've told her that my "money" was only an illusion, a way of deceiving everyone, including myself.

"Nice to meet you," I said, shaking her mother's hand.

"I'll take care of your daughter tonight, promise," I told them, gripping her father's hand, thinking that both of her parents looked just like Odie.

Odie's father tightened his grasp when he said, "You also need to behave with my daughter. I don't want to hear anything that I don't want to hear. And you know what I don't want to hear, when I say I don't want to hear it, right?"

Odie interrupted, "Dad, *stop*!"

Her parents then wished us a good time and asked that I'd bring her home at a reasonable hour, which meant we'd have to abbreviate dinner and miss dessert and coffee, especially if we planned on rolling around in the sheets.

We waved a big goodbye to everyone as we backed out of the driveway. Nick and Jojo jumped up and down, screeching, "We'll miss you!"

At that point, I was under the assumption that this was a perfect family, and it wouldn't be until years later that Odie would disclose the backstory of her father and his tendency to drink, and how this affliction deeply affected her family. She'd opened up to me only after I began to let her in on my problems. The more I spoke about my life the more she'd reveal of hers. The trouble is most people go to their grave with their secrets, and for that reason they'll have to suffer all the more.

27

CIGARETTES & DOGS

I just sat down in front of the computer to write. I have an hour or so to put some thoughts together. And before Odie gets home, I have to go pick up dinner. She's in a meeting that's running late and Madison is eating pizza at her friend's house. I try to make use of these bits of time, and write while I can.

I want to write more about the first time I met Odie's parents, but there's not much here in the journals to go by, and I can't remember anything else. I'm exhausted and thinking about giving up. I worked all day. And now I've been staring at this same page of my journal for a half hour which reads: *"Old man is where?"* There's nothing else on the page besides this. What does it even mean? I cross out this phrase and write in its place:

"I'm right here."

Outside, through the front window, I see a young, nervous-looking guy walking his dog. I've never seen him before. He's smoking a cigarette, talking on his telephone. His dog pulls at the chain, but the guy is extremely engaged with his phone call as if something dire was transpiring during this conversation. I try to imagine what he's saying. Then the man just smiles.

Sitting on the curb, I see my father smoking a pipe. He blows smoke circles into the air. Each wispy ring settles to the concrete, vanishing.

I stand up and tap on the glass.

I have nothing to offer today. I want to write more but there's nothing.

28

TWIN TOWERS, BLUE BALLS & ARSENIO HALL

Odie and I were off to City Island for our first date together, and I thought it would be a good idea to drive over the Whitestone Bridge to catch the bright city skyline. My father would've appreciated that I was acting as the tour guide that man had an eye and heart for all things beautiful, all things New York.

"This is a nice view, huh?" I said. The horizon stretched with jagged concrete teeth that shot up into the sky, a world built by ambition, meant to last. A plane soared overhead and I reached out to hold her hand.

"It's too pretty. Makes you forget yourself for a minute," she said. I liked the way she said things. She had a gift for making the ordinary sound profound. Each time I tried to reciprocate the conversation it felt forced.

"You see the Towers over there?"

"I do. I've actually never been there before."

"They're really amazing. My father showed me this view a long time ago," I said.

"Well, tell your father when you see him next that I said he's got good taste." I wanted to say, "My father's dead," but I said nothing.

At the restaurant, I forget the name of it now, the lights were low, and our waiter, who resembled Arsenio Hall, with those big delicate eyeballs, was eyeing Odie's breasts the whole time we ate. To be honest, I couldn't blame the guy as I couldn't help myself either. The way her breasts collected in that dress made you want to bury your head in there and take a quick nap. But this jerk kept coming back to fill up Odie's water and after the third refill I was about to say something. I decided not to, because the night was going so well: the candlelight, the conversation, the good food. I began to think that maybe I didn't need coke or booze to have a good time after all.

"Do you want a glass of wine?" I asked.

"Sure. What should we get? I don't know wines at all," she said, smiling.

"I'm okay, actually. But you should have one." She liked that I wasn't drinking.

We laughed right through dinner. Odie even tried baked clams for the first time.

Then it was dessert, on to coffee, leaving plenty of time to get home at a reasonable hour.

On the way back, riding over that bridge again, I pulled out an early victory cigar. I was going to get my end in, I thought.

"Do you mind if I have a cigar?" I asked.

"Doesn't bother me, I don't care."

"Are you sure? I don't mind if I don't."

"You should. I like the way they smell. I always have, even when I was a kid."

"Do you want one then? I have two."

"I guess I should," she laughed.

We smoked those things and watched the city sparkle like a giant casino. She grabbed my thumb, and held on for the entire ride. I wanted to tell her I loved her, but I didn't know her. Instead, I said, "Do you want to come back to my house?"

She didn't answer me.

"We don't have to do anything you wouldn't want to do, promise. Or anything your father wouldn't want to hear?" There was a pause, and it was long enough that I now knew I'd be riding home alone with my meat-cock between my hands.

Then she spoke, "Okay. But take me home first." If I had another cigar I would have lit it right there. Though I have to admit, I was surprised she said yes, especially after what her father said to me. I wasn't going to question it. But as a father now who has a young daughter, I would *never* let my twenty-year-old sleep at a strange man's house after their first date, because I know there are people out there just like me waiting to get on any girl they can.

So I brought her to her house, and she was in and out within five minutes, swinging a pink duffle bag around her shoulder. She hopped into the car, smiling. She wanted me to undress her right there, I thought.

"This is good. This is going to be good," I said to myself.

When we got back to my place I could tell she was overwhelmed.

"I can't believe this is all yours," she said, walking around. She was used to living with six or seven other people in a cramped apartment, and here I had my own spot with multiple spacious rooms. Yet I wasn't about to tell her that my aunt gave me this apartment for nearly nothing.

"It's really great." She inspected all three bedrooms, the gym, the bathroom, the backyard, the living room, the kitchen, everywhere. She liked the wall-to-wall carpeting, the vibrant pastel colors of each room, the rose printed furniture, and that big screen TV.

"I'm glad you like it." I held her hand, rubbing the inside of her palm.

Odie then went into the bathroom to get changed, while I sat on the bed waiting to be mauled by this Cuban princess. I was as big as a leg when she came out in skin-tight shorts and a tank top with no bra. I almost cried.

"You're too much," I said. She walked right past me and went under the covers.

"Good night, Bernard." I went to kiss her neck when she pushed my hand off.

"What's the matter?"

"Bernard, you said we didn't have to do anything that I didn't want to do."

"You're playing, right?"

"Good night, Bernard." She leaned over and turned off the light. I wanted to kick the wall but held back just in case this was a test or maybe she'd change her mind.

Within five minutes she was asleep, and I was left staring up at the ceiling in disbelief. A few minutes later, the neighbors next door started riding each other like psychotic coyotes. I couldn't take it. I had to end this. I got up and went into the bathroom and started rubbing one out. And then for whatever reason I remembered I never called my mother. She was probably worried, and here I was yanking one out, and now I couldn't get my mother's damn face out of my head. I had to stop for a second. This was ridiculous, I had to try and think of someone else.

Outside the bathroom window, I now heard some random couple shouting at each other, which didn't help the mood either. I was desperate when I heard an urgent knock at the door. It was Odie, here to relieve me.

"Bernard? Are you going to be long? I have to pee."

"I'll be right out. Okay. Be right out."

"Is someone fighting outside?"

"Be right out."

I started up again. I had to finish but it wasn't working. I was moving as fast as I could, burning the head.

"Bernard! Please! I'm going to pee all over the floor."

And there I was on our first date: my pants snaked about my ankles, the coyotes heaving upstairs, the neighbors exchanging obscenities on the pavement, while some gorgeous Cuban prude was about to piss all over my apartment.

"I'll be right out. Just give me a minute. Okay?"

"Bernard, I'm going to pee everywhere." I couldn't finish. I opened the door, and she rushed past me, telling me to get the hell out.

"Close the door!" she demanded.

I don't think I slept that night, not because of my leg-size dick, but because something felt different, something felt good. I met my wife that night.

29

ODIE SAYS

Odie says we never went back to my place after our first date. She says she would've never done that. Her parents would've killed her, and she would never lie to them about something like that.

I believe her. But that's not how I remember it.

30

TACOS, VACATION & FEELING OLD

Tonight, Odie and I looped around the block to get some tacos. The moon was out and Madison was at her new friend Julie's house for a sleepover.

"I want to quit my job," Odie said.

"Okay," I said.

"No, I'm serious. Don't say 'okay' like that."

"How do you plan on us affording that? People are getting fired nowadays and begging for a job and you're quitting?"

"I don't know. But I'm quitting. I can't take it, and I want to be home with Madison."

She rolled down the window, and stuck her head out the window.

"What the hell are you doing?" I asked, but she didn't hear me. She had half her body outside.

When she came back in she said, "Where do you want to go on vacation this year?

Have you thought about it anymore?"

"I don't know. Not really." We pulled up the drive thru.

"What are you getting?" I asked.

"Just a burrito supreme."

"Nothing else?"

"And a nachos. Nachos supreme. And a taco."

"That's it? A burrito and nachos and a taco."

"All supreme," I said.

We drove into an empty diner parking lot to eat. We sat under the tall incandescent lights, where crowds of bugs were attacking the bulbs. They would blindly smack into the plastic over and again.

"Do you think I look old?" Odie asked. "Bernard? What are you looking at?

Bernard!"

"Nothing. Just those dumb bugs. What'd you say?"

"I asked you if you thought I looked old."

"What are you talking about? You look beautiful."

"But am I old looking? That was the question I asked. I feel old, today."

"Then maybe tomorrow you won't feel old. Can you hand me my chicken taco?"

"Why do we even eat this crap when we know it's going to kill us?"

"It's quick, what do you mean? Why are you asking that while we're eating it? You handed me the wrong taco. You handed me the beef taco. I want to eat the chicken one first."

"What's wrong with Madison?"

"There's nothing wrong with her. Why would you say that?"

"I don't know. I never had any trouble with school. It was easy for me. What are we doing wrong with her?"

"Well, she's not you. And it's not for you to get. And not everyone is meant to go to Columbia University."

She looked at me. "Maybe there's nothing wrong." She ate a few nachos. "Oh, before I forget, tomorrow I'm going to Diane's house to get my haircut. I have to get it cut for this presentation on Monday morning. So can you pick up Madison then?"

"I guess so. I was planning on working on the book, but sure. What time?"

"When are you going to be finished with the book already?"

"Soon."

"You've been writing it forever. How long has it been? I don't even know." She took a big bite out of her burrito. "Where do you want to go on vacation this year?" she said, chewing.

"I don't know. Where do you? What'd you say, France or Italy? I would go there, if that's what you want to do. Or Haiti sounds nice, too."

"These nachos are soggy," she said. "Oh, Bill stopped by yesterday by the way. I forgot to tell you. He needed to borrow your sander. I didn't know where it was. That guy freaks me out."

"Yeah, he's a pain in the ass. But he's lonely, too. I feel bad for him."

"Well, you definitely seem to talk to him a lot. It seems you spend more time with him than me."

"That's not true. And I don't talk to him that much. What are you talking about?"

"I'm ready for my next taco."

I rubbed my hand inside her thigh.

"Bernard, what the hell are you doing? We're in a parking lot."

"Exactly. I was trying to be romantic. Remember when we were young?"

"I thought you just told me that I wasn't old?" She huffed, "My taco, *please*."

"Let's go home then and..." I tried rubbing her leg again.

"Bernard, I'm tired. I worked all day. Can I get my taco, I said."

It's the small things these days, time found within the daily tumult, that now seem like major victories.

31

MEMORY BEGINS ELSEWHERE, DREAMS ETC.

Sometimes I wake to the small sounds of our room, first light skims the wall, the ceiling, onto the floor, dust swims over me and I'm born once more. I look over at Odie and she's still here. I've done nothing wrong, this life can't be wrong, these nightmares hold nothing over me, and so I write them all down. Though the more I go back to that final moment with my father, the more I wish I'd just held his hand.

The problem is I no longer remember that last instance with the old man as it was. It now appears as a mixture of all the dreams and memories, making it impossible to relive that final goodbye. Last night, it was the old man with his tongue torn out, and in its place were blood-soaked cotton balls, as Odie sat in the corner, smoking two cigars at once, while that whistling doctor, wearing a peacock hat, gave it to her, driving his hips.

"The front hole," Odie said, giggling. "The front hole." I looked back at the bed and there was Madison, Odie, Isabella, and Mom asleep in my father's bed. Bill was in the corner of the room watching, tapping his hand against the wall.

"Tap, tap, tap, tip, tap," Bill said. "Got to love those drums!"

And last week, Cosby and my father jerked each other off into the Jell-O cups left over from a hospital lunch.

"Don't get it on the floor, poppies. And don't kick any nurses today, okay?" Cosby said.

My father smiled. "Promise," he said, cradling a severed Panda's head, worms blossoming, wriggling from its bloody neck.

But these dreams occupy my waking life, too, which makes it hard to separate what's fact from fake, when I'm at work, when I'm eating dinner with my family, when I'm driving in the car. The other day, I thought I almost drove over this boy skipping over the road, clutching a luggage bag and a spray of sunflowers. I turned the wheel, swerving out of the way, almost onto oncoming traffic.

Odie shouted, "What the hell are you doing?"

"I didn't want to hit that boy."

"What boy?"

After that incident, Odie insisted that I talk to a professional to sort this out.

"Bernard, this is out of control."

She even went so far as to bring it up to my mother and my sister, and they suggested I see someone too. Just yesterday, my daughter Madison ran into the kitchen, as I was pressed up against the sink, the window sill, searching the yard for this blue bird that flashed from branch to branch, when I saw the suicide jumper pull himself back up from the ledge.

Madison then tapped me and I almost whacked her in the head, thinking it was him, when I realized it was my little girl with her backpack, smiling out from those curls.

I couldn't speak. Sometimes I can't. I'm not as attentive as I should be. I'm just not here. And if she has problems with her friends or with school and she needs someone to talk to, well, sometimes I just miss. These days I'll see her face, full of light, and realize how capable I am, as her father, of wrecking her delicate mind. One misstep and she could carry the burden of her father's faults for the rest of her life.

"Dad, who are you talking to?" she asked.

I said nothing. The bird hopped down to the grass.

"Daddy, stop!" she whined, jumping up and down, when she punched my thigh, I woke.

"Madison. Don't do that. You don't hit."

"But you're ignoring me, Da-aad."

"You don't hit though. Okay?" She didn't respond, so I asked her, "Did you get your lunch out of the fridge?"

"Uh-huh," she said. "I hate school, Dad."

"Why do you hate school?"

"I just hate it."

"Is there something you like about it?"

"I like lunch. I don't want to go."

"But you have to go."

"I don't want to!"

"You have to. It's important. And I promise one day you'll like it. And Mom and Dad will help you with whatever you need."

She just looked at me.

I added, "Come on, let's walk you down to the bus stop, kiddo."

And she's already out the door. The only thing more important than the truth, I think, is family.

32

TIME OBLITERATES MEMORY & DAVY CROCKETT

I pulled out that Davy Crockett photo again. The more I look at this picture the more I don't recognize these people. It's like I'm staring at nothing, nothing but a piece of paper. But why can't I remember any of this? It seems time just obliterates memory, especially when your head's been clawed at by years of abuse. But I suppose no one remembers their life as a whole. Instead, it's observed as a run of fragments, something like glass that's been struck to pieces. In the past few years, ever since life began to reveal itself with meaning,

I've tried to put those shards back together to form at least a semblance of a whole image. The problem is most of what's been reassembled doesn't appear complete; it's as if I'm looking at a thousand different images at once.

33

COPACABANA, GARFIELD, & ODIE MOVES IN

For some reason I remember this one chic bar called the Copacabana. It was around the block from the Pierre, and considered to be one of the "hot spots" in the 90's. Each night this place was jammed with celebrities and hotel-heads from all over: the Plaza, Sherry Netherlands, and any other spot you can think of. We'd drown the place out right after our shift lifted. Good music, better food, and a library of drinks, where more than likely you'd stumble upon a shuffle of stars milling about: Russell Simmons, Mick Jagger, maybe even Cindy Crawford (or was it Kathy Ireland?), Darryl Strawberry, Morton Downey Jr., Martin Sheen, Billy Crystal, Kevin Spacey maybe, and flocks more. We drank the same drinks as the stars.

The night after my first date with Odie, I thought I'd celebrate, so I sunk into a few drinks with my good friend Joe. I was in a great mood. But back then I couldn't handle being happy. Anytime things went well I'd go out of my way to blunt that feeling, to forget myself.

Joe said, "I hooked up this one ass-face today. He needed some valium or some shit.

But I hooked it up. And you know what? I got jack-shit in return. I hate my fucking job."

"This other goddamn lady, she just moved in, she takes her dog every day for swimming lessons. What's wrong with these people? Don't they know that dogs already know how to swim?" I said.

"Yeah, everyone knows that about dogs."

"Hey, get this. I had this date last night with this Cuban girl I just met," I said.

"Okay."

"It was amazing."

"Amazing, huh?"

"We smoked cigars, drove through the city. She ate clams for the first time. I brought her home on the first date. She got into these tiny little shorts. We fucked like champions all night." Although it didn't happen this way, it still felt right to say it. "Did she whistle before she came?" Joe asked.

"What the hell does that mean?"

"Well, was she a good hit?"

"Yeah, sure she was. She's like a fucking serpent between the sheets. And she's only 20," I said.

"So you're telling me you're hitting a little girl that behaves like a snake?"

"I meant 25…24 or 25. Yeah, and we had clams and cigars too."

"Yeah, you just told me that."

Joe had to leave after his first drink when Mickey showed up howling his head off, waving a ticket across the air. I couldn't understand him at first because he spoke too fast. "I won. I fucking won. I won two and half million dollars. Fuck you, you fuckers." There were tears in eyes and his voice was so high it seemed his head was about to split. He hugged me and then pulled out his wallet and put a hundred dollar bill on the bar and told the bartender, "Drinks on me tonight! Drinks on fucking me!" I wanted to punch him in the smile and I didn't know why. It was my turn to speak, I thought. I wanted to tell everyone about Odie, my "lotto ticket," and how I got laid three times last night.

But everyone gathered around Mickey and we all listened to every word he said.

"I fucking told that asshole Hiro and his little bitch Phillip that I quit. I fucking quit. They can go eat my dick. I'm done. The Pierre is done. I'm fucking done! I'm out. I'm finally fucking free of those assholes!"

We all held our shots up. Mickey was the hero of the moment, and so we sang: "To Mickey!" And I bet the rest of the bar probably thought we were all best friends. "To Mickey!"

Then somehow I ended up across the room with this bellboy Miles from the Plaza Hotel. I lost track of Mickey, and now that I think about it, I was probably jealous. I craved what he had. I just didn't know it. And that would be the last time I'd ever see Mickey.

So Miles and I ordered a few shots and I was jawing away, again:

"Champions, that's how we fucked all night. She's like a crazed rattle snake or some kind of snake bitch in bed. She's got these tight shorts and she spoke Spanish to me most of the night. We ate seafood too. Do you want another drink, Joe? We went over some bridges, yeah. She blew me in the car on the way to the restaurant, a pre-date blow job, and then another big wet nice blowie on the way back. And yeah, I met her parents, too, who looked just like her—just not as hot. We fucked all night. Odie and I did, that is. Not the parents. We went at it till the sun came up. Did I say that already?" We grabbed a few more shooters, and I hit up the bathroom for a line or two just to sober up a bit.

"What's her name, B?" Miles asked.

"Odie."

"Like the dog Odie? Like Garfield's Odie? Did this snake bark too? Just curious."

"Not like the dog Odie, asshole. A different Odie. This Odie is hot as fuck. She's twenty-nine years old at least."

"So now you're banging the old dried-out ladies, huh, B?"

"I meant twenty years old. She's twenty years old and she doesn't look like a dog you fuck-nut."

"You better be careful with that bait. She'll be moving into your place before you know it."

"Are you kidding me? Moving in! Hah! You're out of your goddamn skull, Miles. You know that? Your goddamn skull. You think I'd let some twenty-year-old move into my apartment?" I dropped my beer on the floor. The glass shattered and I tried to pick up the pieces but the bartender raced over and told me that I'd hurt myself if I did that. I handed over what I'd already picked up and he shook his head, and said, "I'll take care of the rest."

But my hand was cut and deeply. I put it into my pocket so no one could see. With my other hand, I took some of the bar napkins and stuffed them into the bloody pocket. Miles then told me he had to leave early too. He had to wake up for work. So I went over to this other guy, Norm, who was the manager at some boutique hotel around the block.

"Can I get you a drink, Norm? Just one more. I'm not drinking that much tonight,

Norm." I reached into my pocket with my good hand and pulled out the last of my tips.

"If you say so, Bernard." Norm was a good listener, a rarity.

"Norm, she's really fucking smart, man. Not like the other girls. And she fucked me on our first night out. How fucking cool is that? The first fucking date and I fucked her."

"That sounds great. Listen, I'm going to head home."

"No, you're not. You can't leave me here. Everyone else has gone home. I'm not staying here alone. You're staying with me, Norm." I looked around at the bar and it was packed.

"I'm just not in the mood tonight, Bernard."

"What are you a pussy or something? Come on, we never, we never, hang out," I said.

Norm asked to borrow my drink. He then grabbed it from me and drank the rest.

"Go home, Bernard. Your hand's bleeding." I'd forgotten. I pushed my hand into my pocket.

129

"What's wrong with you, Norm?"

"How about this Bernard, are you ready? How about my brother died last week?

Does that work for you? Is that reason enough for me to want to go home?"

"So you are going home?" I became depressed and didn't know why. "Is that even true? You're tugging my dick, right?" I asked.

"Go home, Bernard, you're too drunk and you need to clean that fucking hand. It's getting all over everything." My pocket had soaked through with blood, and there was some on my dress shirt.

The bartender pulled Norm aside and spoke to him. But I could hear every word he said: "Norm, you need to get this guy a cab. And someone's got to pay his tab."

"I'll take care of it," Norm said.

"I'm still staying for a while," I demanded. "I told you that already. I'm not going home. Why would I go home?"

"Come on Bernard, we're going to get you a cab."

"Is that an insult, Norm? Don't attack me, Norm. I know you're upset about your brother, but I see what you're doing to me, big guy. I see it."

"What the hell is wrong with you?"

"You don't think I can handle my shit? All you people. And all you people are the delusional ones."

Norm interrupted my rant and told me he'd be right back, that he had to use the "little boys' room." After a half hour it was obvious Norm wasn't coming back. So I was left to argue with the bartender about the bill. I showed him my empty pockets, when he finally threatened to call the police.

I then stood up on a bar stool and called out: "Get one of these rich bastards to pay for it. These people should pay for it. Not the poor asshole. Get Mickey to pay for it. He's rich now that fucking bastard." I raised my empty glass into the air.

"Sit down you big old dick! You're ruining my goddamn night," someone called out.

"Do you know who I am?" I demanded.

"Yeah, you're a fucking loser with a bloody hand and a big mouth," another person said.

"Do you know I am?"

"Buddy, sit the fuck down. Nobody gives a shit who you are." He held his drink up and said, "And after this one, I'm not even going to remember ever seeing you for that matter."

I went at it again. "You think your money makes you virtuous? You're all as miserable and empty as I'll ever be. Every last one of you. And hey guess what there assholes…my great grandfather was the President of Haiti. That's fucking right, I'm fucking royalty, so fuck you," I said to anyone who'd listen. There are moments not worth remembering, and perhaps that's one of them.

Someone in the bar yelled out, "Sit down, you drunk ass."

Another guy interjected, "Take your moaning elsewhere, loser."

Then the bartender said, "I'm going to call the police. You need to pay your tab and get lost."

But I had no money left, though I was lucky because one of those "rich bastards" Morton Downey Jr. overheard my tirade and decided to pick up my bill without asking. I suppose there are good people left in this world, and somehow after Morton bailed me out I must've made it home that night. I'm almost certain that my sister Isabella and her Guido boyfriend picked me up that night. She'd rescued me a few times during those decadent years, always when I was too high or drunk to make it home by myself. Isabella was two years younger but sometimes she'd speak to me as if she were my older sister. Once she came to pick me up at the Pierre after I'd stayed overnight for a couple of days. I couldn't leave the building because I was too paranoid, too coked up to go anywhere. Hiro reassured me that there was no one waiting outside the room to drag me back to Haiti.

"Bernard, there's no one there. You need to go home. You have a shift tomorrow afternoon," Hiro said. It was the first time he acted like a boss outside of work.

"I'm not going out there, Hiro. No." I remember I kept thinking about that poor bastard who'd jumped off the building a few months before, and how maybe he had it all right. Jumping meant you were no longer afraid.

"Bernard, it's time to go home, man. The sun is up already. You're acting ridiculous."

"Are you going to fire me Hiro? You're going to fire me, aren't you?"

"I'm not going to fire you. Just get your ass up."

I don't remember much else. Sometime later Isabella picked me up.

That night at the Copacabana, when Isabella drove me home, no one said a word the whole way back. I don't know if she was disappointed or if I was just too incoherent to talk, but we said nothing. I only looked at the back of her long, penny brown hair. She turned her bright face around every so often, just to make sure I was all right. I think I opened the window a few inches, hoping to grab a waft of cool air. Those damn street lights and cars whirred by and I could hear a train patter beyond the apartments. My head spun. Maybe it was better that we rode in silence because I didn't want her boyfriend to listen to our conversation, even though I was anxious to tell Isabella all about Odie. She would've been happy for me. We were always close, especially as kids, and it wasn't until I started to dabble with cocaine that any distance developed.

When we pulled up to my apartment her boyfriend said with his affected Brooklyn accent: "Hurry up with this, will ya. I want to get home for SNL already. Stern is hosting tonight, and it starts up in twenty minutes, so hurry on up."

I stared at the back of his neck. I wanted to punch him.

"I'll be a minute. I just want to make sure he gets in okay," Isabella said.

He then said, "He'll be fine. You need to stop being this guy's mother, you're not his mother." I wanted to punch him in the head.

Isabella opened the car door for me. She was mad but I don't think her anger was directed toward me. She walked me to my room. I think I fell a few times on the steps leading up.

"Are you okay? Do you want me to stay?" she asked.

"You miss Dad at all?" I asked. We walked in and I went to the fridge to get a beer.

"What?"

"It's just a question, that's all. Do you think Mom's okay? Shouldn't we call her to tell her we're both okay? I'll call her right now."

"It's 3 AM, Bernard. What are you doing? You can't keep this shit up much longer." I always admired her candor; it's something I'm incapable of.

"Did you lock the door on the way in? I forgot to lock it. I should go double-check. I don't want anyone to get in here. I'll check." I stood up and walked toward the door.

"I'll lock it on the way out. Bernard, just slow down."

"Do you want a drink? I'm going to drink." I walked into the kitchen and opened a beer.

"You should just get some rest. Why is your hand bleeding? Bernard, why are you bleeding?"

I put my hand back in my pocket. "Oh, you have to, have to meet Odie. Did Ma tell you about her?"

"I don't know what you're talking about."

"She's a good one. A nice one. You should meet her someday."

"Okay, I will. That's fine. Just get in bed."

"I want you to meet her finally. You'd like her, I think."

"Okay, now let's just go to bed. Your eyes look crazy. What did you take?"

I said nothing to her and we just looked at each other and all I could think of was how did I end up here? And then I don't remember anything after that.

To be straight, there was a distinct period from my childhood into my early twenties when Isabella revered anything I did, but as the partying progressed I could sense her appreciation dwindling.

And I think the most serious blunder came when I missed this one Thanksgiving dinner and blamed it on a faulty alarm clock and a headache. The truth was I had been up all night with this big black woman I'd met in the subway and we blew through at least a bag and two bottles of tequila.

That next afternoon, Isabella called:

"Bernard, where the hell are you?"

"I'll be there. Just give me twenty minutes, half hour. Give me an hour," I said. "Why is your voice like that? What are you on? " she asked.

"I'm on my bed. What are you talking about? I'm here on my bed. Why do you accuse me all the time? I told you I have a headache." The girl tried to lick my eyeball, giggling in the phone.

"Who's that laughing? Who's laughing?"

"There's no one laughing, Izzie."

"I need you in me," said the girl in to my ear, loud enough for Isabella to hear.

"Who are you with? You're killing your mother, Bernard," Isabella said.

"There's no laughing, I said. I'm alone. And I told you I have a headache."

"Happy Thanksgiving, Bernard."

After that one phone call, Isabella never gave me the same respect. There are only so many mistakes and lies that you can exhaust before the people around you shut down, turn away. And after a few more slipups, a legitimate fear overtook our relationship, and it was all encompassing, occupying almost every moment, and it wasn't until years after, when I finally cleaned up, that we could begin again, as brother and sister. To this day, however, whenever I sense a distance cropping up between us, when life gets in the way, I have to think it's a direct result of those decadent years.

Two weeks after our first date Odie was sleeping over every night, and with six other Cubans trampling her house she never went back home. The move was sudden and it wasn't until three months into the relationship that I finally got my end in. It was a mindfuck. She wore those tight shorts to bed almost every night. I tried to explain to her that the occasional bump was good for the soul, and how tugging one out every day was what teenagers did.

But when Odie's chastity collapsed, the shorts were torn off, and we went at it all night. Time was dead. We were the moment: the past was a slur, the present only pleasure, and the future, well, whatever.

After we finished, I leaned over and kissed her neck and told her, "My father's dead."

She said nothing and within six quick months she was perched over a bowl, vomiting and pregnant.

I called my mother the day after we found out and probably said something like this:

"Ma, yeah, we'll get married. I promise. Eventually, Ma, don't worry. Don't worry, okay?"

I was going to be a father, a father like my father, I hoped.

34

NO CHILD FORGETS THEIR PARENT'S DEATH

No matter what effort we put forth, however great, we fail. Just like that dancing blue light that's left over after you stare into the sun, but only this image, this ache, floats about for as long as you can go on living with it.

35

THROWING ROCKS AT DUCKS & THE SUN'S DYING

This morning my family and I decided to go on a sunset stroll by a lake nearby. Odie said she needed to get out of the house. She can't handle her boss anymore, she said. Plus, she wants to spend more time with her family. She feels her life is moving away from her, and all she has is a paycheck to show for it.

"I should be home with my daughter and my family."

"I don't disagree."

"Okay."

"But how are we going to make up the hundred thousand dollars a year?"

"So then you do disagree?"

This morning the urgency to get out was even greater because that drummer around the block was banging away at his kit.

"How is this happening this early? Am I hearing things? Why hasn't anyone else said something? We should just call the police."

"You're not hearing things. But we're not calling the cops. You can't tune it out?" "Let's get out of here. I want to get out of the house now. I can't stand it."

After we were able to get Madison away from the computer for a minute, we went for a walk. It was the first walk I remember taking in a long time, maybe since we moved in ten years earlier. The neighborhood looked different at this pace: the matching green lawns, sprinklers clacking, windows darkened by curtains, laundry floating in the air, dogs flaunting their teeth through fences, as a train echoed beyond the rooftops.

As we circled the water, Odie said, "You look exhausted again, Bernard." She let go of my thumb.

"Yeah, I didn't sleep too well last night." What did she want to know? That last night my father sat up in bed, and I punched his eye over and again, when a swarm of bees spilt out of his ears.

"Bernard, you're going to get yourself sick."

"I was just up late last night."

She looked disturbed but concerned. "Bernard, what's going on?" she grabbed my hand.

"Nothing. I'm fine." I smiled but I wasn't okay, the past was always there now.

The ducks scattered, quacking, as we approached, when Madison asked, "Dad, can I quit school?"

"Why do you want to quit school?" Odie looked at me.

"It's boring and I hate words."

The fatherly advice I should've offered her eluded me. And before I could summon an answer she was already ten feet head throwing rocks at some nearby ducks, and it sounded like a full-on duck war had overtaken the park.

Madison threw another. The water rippled, circles grew outward until they were shapeless rings, and I looked at Odie's thin, wavering reflection that undulated along the lake's surface, trying to catch a glimpse of her expression. I couldn't tell what she was feeling. The she yelled at Madison. "Madison, don't do that, sweetie!"

She didn't hear Odie as she skipped ahead almost out of eyeshot. She then threw a few more rocks.

"Will you take care of this?" Odie demanded.

"What?" I looked at the ducks.

"Make her stop now."

"She's having fun. Nobody's getting hurt."

"Throwing rocks at ducks? How's that fun? Maybe that's why she's not doing well in school. Because we're not tough enough with her."

"They're only little rocks."

"So if they were big rocks you'd make her stop?"

"Come on, I've seen a lot worse. Look, she's missing them anyhow. She can't throw that far."

Madison was slinging a rock as fast as she could pick one up. Each attempt fell short, sending the ducks quacking into the air, feathers everywhere, only to land a few feet from the attack. It seemed these ducks had no recollection of the prior incident. Madison would then chase in their direction and throw another rock and the process would repeat over and again.

"Maybe we should throw little rocks at you, Bernard, and see how it feels," Odie said.

"That would probably hurt."

It's always been a challenge scolding my daughter for anything she's done that might be considered "wrong" in the eyes of the "moral" world. After you'd spent half your life doing things "wrong," some of which is so far removed from what the rest of the world considers appropriate, it becomes somewhat of a task to enforce "rules" upon anyone else. *The kid can do whatever she wants,* is how I think about it. Odie too can be ruthless at times but I can never gather the courage to tell her she is "wrong," or that she's hurting my feelings. I've been "wrong" my whole life and because of it everyone else will forever be "right." And I'll never be able to say what I want, when I want. And I've come to accept that.

Odie pressed, "She's going to hit one. Bernard, just go tell her to stop. There are people around watching. Do you want people to think your daughter is psychotic?"

"What does it matter, anyhow, if she hits one? Who cares, right? Nothing matters," I laughed. "The sun is dying, right, and the universe is still expanding, Odie. Am I right?"

"What the hell are you talking about? What do you mean the sun's dying? We're all dying, Bernard. But right now, your daughter is throwing rocks at the ducks and you're talking about how the sun is dying? You make feel like I'm crazy sometimes. Just go get your daughter and let's go home."

"That was your idea. You don't remember? You told me when we first met that the sun was going to disappear one day. And that means we'll disappear too?"

"I don't know what you're talking about, Bernard. I guess I'll just have to do it myself." Odie had forgotten our first conversation in the park, as she waltzed ahead, catching up with Madison. She then made Madison put the rocks down and gave her a big hug.

36

PREGNANCY & THE MISCARRIAGE

Odie glowed those first few months of pregnancy. She was the mom-to-be and I was supposed to be the overjoyed father. Everything was in its proper place, seamless, and somehow I still couldn't tune in. Then the real problems came, when she had her first miscarriage a few months into the pregnancy. She was devoured by grief, and I became a slither, a ghost, I wasn't there for her. She blamed herself over and again. And I remember the exact moment when we first found out, the blood in the toilet and that guttural sound that shouldn't come from such a delicate girl.

"No, no, no!" she bawled.

The more she suffered, hollering from room to room, the less I could listen.

For weeks after, Odie refused to leave the bed. She hardly ate or showered or changed her clothes. But I tried to block it out. By day, I was hustling for tips, and at night I was usually at some all-hours soiree, where most nights I never made it home, and things only got worse. She quit school not too long after that, and once I even found her asleep in the bathtub in her jeans and sweatshirt.

"Odie! What are you doing?" I shook her, raising her out of the tub.

"You're no good. I could've loved you," she slurred.

I begged her to tell someone else what happened just so I didn't have to take on the burden alone.

"You should tell your mom or something." I would've called her parents but they didn't like me back then, because we lived together unmarried.

One time our neighbor Alex knocked at our door, and asked us to quiet down because his baby was trying to sleep. Odie and I had been arguing all morning about who drank the last of the orange juice, and when I didn't get the answer that I wanted, I poured a gallon of milk onto the kitchen floor. Odie growled and tore out a handful of her hair, which floated to the floor.

Alex came just as the hair settled into the milk. When I opened the door he was standing in his bathrobe. "What are you doing in there anyway? My kid can't sleep," he said.

"Not sure," I said. I wanted to jam his eyes out with my thumbs. He didn't know how lucky he was to have a kid.

"You don't know what you're doing in there? What's all the screaming about?"

"We're watching TV. The TV is loud. I'll turn it down."

He smirked and said, "Yeah, why don't you do that then."

To be fair, though, it wasn't always this bleak. There were good days, too. Days that appear with no meaning, when time just happens, but these recollections seem to be the most difficult to call up, the most fragmented. But there were afternoons when we'd drift through the park arm-in-arm. Or our first vacation in Montauk. Or when we'd visit each other's parents for a Sunday dinner, or when we'd get a quick bump in the morning before work.

"Please, one more time," she begged one time.

"You're a lunatic. I have to go to work."

"Either you put it in here again or I'm going home for good."

"Put it where?" I asked.

"In this hole, right here," she said, pointing to the tangle of hair between her legs.

"What hole?" I laughed.

"The front hole, you ass."

Her cheeks blotched, and I only wish I could remember more. And the irony is that without much effort I can still visualize going at it with some frizzy call-girl or banging through a sloppy rail off a $30,000 diamond table—all of that comes back too easily.

37

3AM

I shot Bill's mouth off tonight. Then my father scolded me for being impulsive and not listening to anyone, ever. Now I'm looking out the bedroom window, the yard looks still under the streetlight. Every home appears static, heavy with sleep, waiting for the next workday. Odie snores a bit, and it's quiet apart from the random car that circles the distance. And I think I just heard raccoons rifling through Bill's garbage. I'm tempted to go downstairs, but I should try to sleep.

38

GOLDFISH CRACKERS & WHY'D YOU MARRY ME?

This afternoon, after waking up late, Odie and I circled the supermarket aisles for a pack of "amazing" Goldfish Crackers that Madison had begged us to pick up. Madison said, "It's like Goldfish Crackers but it's not. They're Space Adventure Goldfish Crackers. Jenny's mom got them yesterday at the supermarket."

When we couldn't find the crackers we asked the store manager, and when he couldn't locate them he asked the stock boy, who told us they just sold out.

"The kids can't get enough," the stock boy said. "They rip them right off the shelves."

"Aren't they just crackers?" I asked.

The stock boy just looked at me as if I were crazy.

When Odie and I got to the checkout line, standing beneath those loud lights, I saw a carton of milk in our shopping cart, and I began to think about that last chapter I'd just written, and how wretched I was to her in the past.

Looking around the store, I tried to forget this memory. The cashiers scanned their items, the cash registers opening, closing, when a woman got on the loud speaker and said there was broken glass in aisle nine. Behind us was a plump woman propped over her cart which was capped off with mayonnaise, cereal, bacon, and I don't know what else. Another lady, who probably hadn't slept in weeks, kept scratching at her eye. What were their problems like, I thought. Then this guy with his nose pierced rolled toward an open register, cheery-eyed, as if acting like a jackass was something to be proud of.

I looked back at Odie. "Odie?" She was absorbed by a magazine. I tapped her on the shoulder. "Odie?"

"What?" she asked.

"Why'd you marry me?"

"What are you talking about?" she said, looking around, embarrassed.

"Why'd you marry me? Why would you do that to yourself?"

"What are you doing, Bernard?"

"I don't get it. Why would you marry me?"

"Because I love you."

"Yeah, but why'd you love me? You knew exactly what I was doing all along. Why'd you stay? And then why'd you ever think to marry me?"

"Really, Bernard?" She looked over at the heavy woman in front of us, who was now waiting on every word we said.

"You could've been with anyone else. You were smart, young, and beautiful. Why'd you put up with me? It makes no sense."

"Right now, I'm not so sure," she said. She then put the magazine back on the rack.

I could tell she was about to cry, but I didn't care. I needed to know.

"Odie?"

"Bernard, I'll just meet you in the car." She handed me our credit card and turned to walk away, when I grabbed her by the shirt.

"Let go of me," she yelled.

"I'm sorry. I just don't understand. I wouldn't have stayed if I were you."

She twisted, and said, "That makes me sad."

The stock boy then came running up to us, shouting, "Hey! I found you our very last Space Adventure Goldfish Crackers!"

THE REVOLVING DOOR

He handed me the box. "Thanks," I said.

Odie just looked at me, shaking her head. "*Our* daughter will be thrilled." She then pushed through the line and ran out the sliding doors.

A day or two went by before Odie spoke to me. I told her I was sorry over and again.

"A supermarket is a not the place for a conversation like that. But I just wanted to talk."

"Now you want to talk?" she said. "After fifteen years and now you want to talk?"

"I guess."

"Well, I don't want to. I'm sorry, I just don't. But to answer your question, I don't know why I married you. I still don't but I did and I have to live with that every day. And now we have a daughter. And so it's no longer about us. And that's all I'm going to say."

"I'm sorry. It's just since I started writing this book, I keep thinking about things.

It's driving me nuts," I said.

"Then maybe you shouldn't be writing this book," she snapped.

There are moments when I feel as if I know nothing about her. She's a stranger in my bed or maybe I'm just the stranger after all these years. And wasn't it only yesterday that I smeared our wedding cake in Odie's face. Didn't we just pick out this house together, and paint these walls together? I've sat at that dinner table night after night, slept in this bed by her side for the last fifteen years, and still I'm always starting again, as if nothing came before.

I looked at Odie. "I wish I knew what to say right now."

A tear slid past the bridge of Odie's nose, and we went back to sleep for a little while, an hour or so, I think, until Madison charged into our room. "Mom, can you make me pancakes!"

There's never enough time to reflect, to understand life's intricacies. And what makes this even more complicated, rather, devastating, is that there once was "substantial" time—when you were young and oblivious to its value—when you could actually consider even the most ordinary aspects of your day. And hours, days would be exhausted, laboring over the pleasures, the worries of your day. Maybe if this gift of reflection wasn't presented so early in life then its absence later on wouldn't be so shattering. Now all I can do is push ahead, blindly believing that what's happened before has no real relationship to what's about to happen next.

39

HULK HOGAN & THE WELCOME BACK JERK CIRCLE

In spite of the heaviness at home after Odie's miscarriage, and the weight I walked around with, the Pierre crew welcomed me back without a shudder or thought otherwise. It was as if I'd never left, and we made up, as children would, the instant I came back. There I was front and center at each linen party. Some nights I'd call Odie and tell her that I had to work late or that I had to stay for an overnight shift. Anything to avoid the grief at home, and whether it was blowing some lines or having some girl's lips wrapped around me, I stayed away.

The first night back, we had a Thanksgiving feast in Schwarzenegger's place. After all the cooking and gorging, we formed this jerk circle around this one girl that the crew met at a strip joint. We decided to stage a bet: the first one to drop their load on her wins. We all put fifty bucks into the pot. They crew called this girl Hulk Hogan because she had the same stringy blonde hair and oily tan skin. When "Hogan" was crowned with this new moniker, she couldn't help but simper, a cherry-face flutter that she maintained throughout the night. She even went so far as to play the part, feigning she was the real Hogan, waving her hand to the ceiling, her hand cupped to her ear to indulge the "crowd" as they delighted in her presence.

"Whatcha gonna do when Hulkamania runs wild on you," she sang, stomping her foot on the sheets below. It was horrible but I was high enough to not care.

And you know I'm not even sure who got the prize money that night or if I even finished. I think I've put that part of the night out of my mind and would like to believe it never happened. However, I do remember that viscous web, that mess that was left, shrouding Hogan's body: her eyes, her hair, her belly, all over. She looked miserable even with that tight urgent smile, while everyone else kept at it, eyes cool and aloof, cheeks puffing like they were blowing out a big birthday cake.

I looked around at the crew. It was obvious to me that we were all just afraid, afraid of living a life that meant nothing. We didn't want to admit to ourselves that we didn't control our own lives, that our lives were only lies, little fictions, stories that distracted us.

Hogan moaned, "Take your fucking fingers out of me before I shit all over them, you moron."

Right then, I wanted to die so I wasn't afraid anymore. And I wanted all of them to die too, so they wouldn't be either.

"I'm sorry. I'm sorry. It's just my thumb, it's only my thumb, Hulk," Jimmy replied, yanking his hand out as if he'd been bit. I felt sorry for him, and maybe it was because I knew that he was just as lost as I was.

When Jimmy stood up I drew him to other side of the room away from everyone.

"Jimmy, you can't let people talk to you that way," I whispered.

"What way, Bernard?" he asked.

"Lower your voice, just lower you voice and I'll tell you."

"I told her it was only my thumb. She believed me I think." He looked at me like a child who gets caught doing something wrong.

"You just don't let other people talk to you that way, that's all."

"Bernard, I don't know what you're talking about. I really don't. I'm not saying you're not right but I just don't know what you mean.

Maybe you should tell Hiro about this. He might know what you're talking about." He wiped his forehead of sweat and smiled.

"No, don't say anything anyone."

"Okay, I won't. Do you mind if I go back to the party now?"

But yeah, the linen-days were over, the joy had vanished, nothing unexpected remained. The images, the sounds, the moods, had been recycled too many times. Yet somehow being here was still better than what was happening at home with Odie furled into a bed of despair, so I made sure I was center stage at every last linen-party thrown. After a few months of this behavior, well, Odie began to wonder and started calling me out on it, and either because of arrogance or sheer stupidity I kept partying.

Thinking about this now, I think subconsciously I wanted our relationship to be over. I wanted to get caught.

40

PRIVATE MAGIC SHOW

I don't know if this is my first memory, maybe I just want it to be, and I'm three-years-old.

My small hands, those feet sprawled out on a carpet alongside a few dozen green plastic army men. A shaft of yellow light reaches into the room, and I watch these dust motes spin, dip through the air. Going nowhere but where my eyes follow, I look on for what seems a long while. I try to catch these dancing particles, but they're always floating just out of reach. The sound of the sun, the sound of the room, and it could be hours or minutes before it ends.

41

MY MOTHER

When I think of my mother, I think of each year spent without my father.

42

MRS. DAVIS & CHINESE FOOD

Dinner time and the rain just stopped. The streets glistened, and I went to drag the garbage cans down to the curb when I saw Mrs. Davis fixed on her lawn, holding a rake, staring at the sky. I was tempted to wait until after dinner because I knew she'd hear me scrape the cans along the pavement, and then ask for some favor. I couldn't help her this time because Odie said the leftover Chinese food would be ready in a minute.

Before I could decide, Mrs. Davis turned toward me and asked, "Donnie, can you help me put my plants in my backyard? They need more sun or they're going to die. I don't want them to die."

"Sure, Mrs. Davis," I said.

When I put her plants on the deck she thanked me. "You're not like the other people around here, Donnie. I actually like you."

"Thank you, Mrs. Davis," I said. There was a long silence, and sometimes I don't know how to behave so I smile—just as a doorman would. "I have to get in for dinner now.

Have a good night, Mrs. Davis."

"It's not nighttime yet. Did we go to the zoo when we were kids, Donnie?"

"Mrs. Davis?"

"Good night, Donnie."

"Good night."

Inside Madison and Odie were already eating, watching Wheel of Fortune. The refrigerator hummed and the phone rang in the distance. It was probably Bill, wanting to know what I spoke to Mrs. Davis about.

"Where'd you go?" Odie asked. "Should we get that?" she asked, nodding toward the phone, but keeping her eyes on the TV.

"No, let's just eat." I had to distance myself from Bill. He's overwhelming. It's too intense. His life was becoming my life. His problems were now mine. And he reminded me of what I didn't want to be, and what I knew could very easily become.

"So where'd you go?"

"Mrs. Davis asked me to help her."

"She ought to pay you for all the work you do."

"She's old, Odie."

Madison put the volume louder.

We eat meals and watch TV, forgetting the conversations we should probably have.

43

ODIE KICKS ME OUT & PUNCHED IN THE THROAT

Maybe now I should tell you about that horrible morning when that dog bit me, when Odie punched me in the throat. I've meandered a lot more than I intended to, and it's taken a long time to get to this point, but I still need to tell this part of the story.

So when I knocked on the door, Odie opened it and stood there stock-still, her bloodlined eyes averting my gaze. I walked inside.

"Do you want me to make breakfast?" I asked.

"Bernard, I want you to pack up your bags and get the hell out!"

Through the window the sun shot out between buildings, birds coiled out of the air conditioner and I had a filthy headache.

"Baby, what are you talking about?" I wanted to sound upset but I was high. "You know what I'm talking about. I want you out now or I'm calling the police." I attempted to take off her bathrobe when she swung and hit my throat.

"What the hell? What, what is that?" I asked. My throat throbbed. I tried to talk. "I work all, all night. This is what you do. A punch in the throat?" I smelled of booze and sex. I had nothing on her.

But still, I reminded her, "Baby, I work all fucking day and this is how you repay me." "Work what? What'd you work, some girl's titties tonight? You're a big fucking child, Bernard. You don't think

I know what's happening, you fuck. That stank-ass pussy is all over your hands and I'm tired of you. You hear me now. I'm tired of you."

She knew everything, I thought. "Odie, Odie, please."

"And I'm here home all the time. All alone, all night. Bernard, we just lost a fucking child. Do you remember that? Where the fuck are you?"

"Odie, I'm right here."

"Right here? Right here? Fuck you, Bernard. I'm calling the cops if you don't leave now."

Odie picked up the phone and dialed. I was being kicked out of my own apartment, after she'd moved in only nine months before. I grabbed the phone and tried to de-robe her, again. But she pulled away and for whatever reason picked up the remote off the table and launched it at the wall. The TV went on, a big-eyed newscaster popped up, stating, "*Researchers say 1 out of every 3 people get cancer before they die.*" We both listened. The drama in our own lives no longer had any impact. "*Researchers say that incorporating fruits and vegetables into your diet 3 times a day will lower your risk by 65 %. And up next*

President Clinton says he wants to resolve the crisis in Serbia peacefully. But he also says the Balkan graveyards are filled with President Milosevic's broken promises and Milosevic needs to heed international concerns. Also stay tuned because we've got the latest on the Congo Civil War where the death toll is now reached 8,835 people already. And then a little later we're going to sit down and talk with Hollywood heartthrob Tom Cruise to see what he does on his ranch when he's not breaking hearts across the country. And also up next Baywatch superstar Pamela Anderson finds a pair of eyeglasses in the refrigerator. See who put them there! All of this and more up next!"

The anchor enunciated each word, every consonant and vowel, when a commercial interrupted his pressing speech. Now the TV showed a bright purple pill meant to combat the blackest of depressions. Before the ad finished, Odie had forced her way into the bedroom, slamming, locking the door behind her.

"Odie, what the fuck? Open the door, Odie, now, please." She didn't answer. I went over to the living room table and picked up her hairdryer. I walked toward the window and threw it outside, watching it turn into the hedges below. To this day I don't know why I did that.

Then I crept up to the bedroom door and sat on the floor. "Baby, please let me in. I didn't do anything. Actually, baby, I didn't want to tell you this but I got bit by a dog today.

No shit. Here, open up and I'll show you. I want you to see the bite."

I thought I heard Odie laughing through the wood paneling. I started to laugh along, but it just felt strained. Then I heard these long muscular sobs.

"Odie please let me in. Please O-die. Listen Odie, I'll get help. I'll check myself into rehab. I'll make this work. I'll get help, just please."

She said nothing. There was nothing.

44

EMPTY ROOM & EMPTY BED

An empty room, the light is low. Red and white lights splash against the window, sirens trail the distance. My father is a pile of sheets. In the corner of the room, a Panda stands, hitting a snare drum with its claws, tilting his head back and forth, and I start anyway: *Dad, remember when we caught those thieves?*

It's cold and damp and I'm in a movie theater, alone, and there are pigeons scattering through the rafters, as I sit and watch this massive screen: an empty room, the light is low.

My father is a pile of sheets. *Dad, remember when we caught those thieves?*

My father sobs over me. I'm dead. He picks the telephone up off the table and throws it at the wall. "My boy, my only boy," he says over and again. "Don't listen to you mother, you never went to the zoo."

My father stands on his bed. "Please, let me die, old boy. Let me die, already," he says. "I want to die. No one should feel this much."

I want to respond but nothing comes.

Standing on the bed, Mrs. Davis, begs, "Please, let me die. Let me die, will you, Bobby, and I'll make you cookies, I swear."

Nothing comes.

Wake up, the light thrums.

Odie shakes me. "Bernard, you're late!"

I was asleep on the toilet.

"Bernard, what the hell are you doing?" she shouts. "You're late for work."

"Yep, okay," I struggle.

I rub the sleep from my eyes. She leans into the mirror and starts painting her lips dark red.

"You're so smart and good, Odie."

"So smart that I've got to go to this damn job every day." She smacked her lips together. "Well, we'll see how long this lasts." She turned to look at me. "And what the hell were you sleeping on the toilet for anyway?"

"I don't know. I guess I had to shit. I have no idea. I don't even remember waking up."

"Did you go over to that house again, like I asked you?"

"I told you I went."

"You never told me that. And if you did then how come it hasn't stopped? It's all the time, Bernard. It's nightmarish. How come no one else has complained yet? Or better yet even shot this person. What about your *boyfriend* Bill? He's not afraid to speak up."

"Stop with that boyfriend crap. And I'm not afraid to speak up. I resent that."

She leaned over and kissed me on the forehead. "Love you. Have a good day.

Hopefully, I won't be home late. Make sure Madison eats her oatmeal. And give her a banana, too. Bernard, are you listening to me?

"A banana, yep, I heard you."

"And oatmeal. Oatmeal and a banana. Not just a banana." She said, kissing me again, and then she was gone.

45

MONSTERS IN MY ROOM

I'm five or six years old and there was this small amber light in my room that liked to flicker and terrorize me. Along the walls and floorboard, creaks and groans would blend with this light show, and eventually this would send me darting down the hallway toward my parents' bedroom as fast as my feet would take me there. My father would then pick me up, place me over his shoulder and bring me back to my bed.

"There are monsters in my room," I said, peeking from beyond his shoulder as we walked to my room.

"Okay, let's go get these monsters out of your room," he said.

He'd help me look around the room for all the "monsters" that either crawled under my bed or into the closet. We'd chase around inspecting every last detail to make sure that each "monster" had left for the night. If there were any left we'd have to "shoot them dead" with our special invisible "monster-pistols."

To accomplish this "dangerous" task it would sometimes take more than a few minutes. But when I was convinced that there were no more "monsters" to be seen, and when my father was satisfied with a job well-done, well, then I'd go back to sleep and forget anything had ever happened. That was until the next night as this near daily occurrence became something I'd anticipate. I ran to my parents' room to spend time with the old man. Those days he worked too much, and his long, sunken expression couldn't deny it.

As of late, I've wondered what my father was like when he was a child, when he was five or six, battling his own monsters. Was he really just like me, like my mother says? And was his father just like him? Will my daughter be like me? Sometimes I'll look at the mirror and see my old man's face come to life just as fast as it disappears. I want to know where his face escapes to. Part of him is still here, I know it, even if I can't see him.

Start once more, will you.

46

MY MOTHER

When I think of my mother, I think of how I've forgotten about her. How I've pushed her aside, burying her right beside the old man, so I wouldn't have to feel anything.

47

BILL LEAVES A MESSAGE

"Bernard, I caught five more raccoons. Also, did you see the news tonight? I was on the local news, old boy! I'm not joshing you. Call me back. Also, I want to tell you about Jenna.

Some new information on that one. You're not going to believe it. But I can't say *what* over the phone with Madison and all. But you get the drift. Call me back as soon as you get this. I see your car from my window. So I hope you're just taking a nap, finally. Oh, one more thing, I heard those drums last night, all night, loud and clear, old boy. And I'm sure you did too. We should do something about this. Out of control. Out of fucking control. Shit! Oh, my bad. Sorry to for the curse words on your machine. Hope Madison doesn't hear this. All right, hope you're not mad at me. Call me."

48

BILL LEAVES ANOTHER MESSAGE

"Hey, everything okay, old boy? You never called me back. I might stop by to see if you are okay. I've called you a bunch now. Why are you not answering your phone? I still need to tell you about what happened, too. Call me back. All right, call me. I'm home, right now. Don't know if I said that already? One more thing, I bought you some coyote urine. You don't have to pay me back. Next time I see you I'll give it to you."

49

REHAB, THE BIBLE, & ARMS LIKE SPAGHETTI

Rehab is strange. No one listens. I did my twenty-eight days. A punch in the throat is as serious as it gets. I knew that if Odie was ever going to take me back this would be the only way. The Pierre was compliant, allowing me a month-long leave of absence to "clean up my act." I told Human Resources that I had a drinking problem and needed to get it under control.

St. Anne's Rehab Center smelled of metal and chemicals. The people here droned on under that drab white-light as if their hearts had been hollowed out by a butter knife. We all had no choice but to talk to each other, each person's misery infected the next. Everyone would manufacture some story, something that tried to outdo everyone else's: "I almost die-die-die-died driving through a Wal-mart on a pou-pou-pou-pou-pou-pound of m-m-m-meth. Fuck, shit, fuck. We set the whole friggin' pl-pl-pl-pl-ace on fire," riffed this one guy Moses. He battled a bad case of Tourette's and gobbled up Tic Tacs all day.

One day after lunch, this Moses guy and I orbited the court yard, when he told me all the sordid details of his life and how he was "tired of everything." He also said, "If you don't feel crazy then you're probably not alive." It took him a long time to get the words out and when he did it felt like he meant every syllable. But each time I went to explain my story he refused to believe me. He said I shouldn't lie *so* much, especially if I wanted people to respect me.

"You're a fu-fu-fu-fu-cking jokester. Joke-jo-jo-jo-jokes are fu-un-un sometimes, sometimes. Not-not-no-not all the ti-i-i-ime," he said.

And a couple of times he told me that I shouldn't care so much about being rich and famous. He said it would kill me even quicker than all those drugs and parties that I liked to bullshit about.

"I'm telling you the truth, man," I said.

"It's okay I-I-I-I-I." He never finished, because we got called in for dinner.

To be honest, I think all the patients or criminals or freaks or whatever found solace in the falsehoods they spouted. It was because these stories had nothing to do with their lives. At least here, within fiction, we could prop ourselves up and pretend our messy realities didn't exist. This was especially true during group meetings, when each patient would introduce their sob-story. It was then that you understood the simplicity of their struggle: each person begging for a chance at love, over and again. And I couldn't help but see myself in all of them.

This one young boy said, "Radios, I'd mostly steal. And I'd eat any drug I could get a hand on. Even once I beat up my Ma, but with my girlfriend's help. I know I shouldn't be telling you this. But I beat her up twice," he said, tearing up. "Maybe in the next life I'll be better at living it."

I knew exactly what he meant.

Another guy said, "I did my drugs, had my fun, and now I'm here and not sure why. You know what I mean? Like I'd still rather have a needle in my arm right now than to have to talk to you people, no offense."

Someone else said, "Once I get out of here I'm off to Hollywood. I'm gonna get my life together and make it, do something before I die. If I'm not famous by next year I'm going to kill myself."

When it was my turn, I cleared my throat and said what I thought I should say: "We'd swing from chandeliers. And I'd go at it with the most beautiful women all night, always in the fanciest beds, right on through the morning. We'd blow lines off each other's bodies until our throats burnt. I've been in Mick Jagger's place, Princess Diana, Michael Jackson, Bill Cosby. It felt right. I liked being me then. I still like being me. But I guess I'm here to find out why other people don't like me being me."

Just when I thought I was being honest, as I felt that pull at my gut, I looked up and saw that everyone in the group had retracted into their own private worlds, not listening to a single word I'd said. I could hear the TV yapping down the hallway and there was Moses jumbling with his Tic Tacs, but that was it.

"Thank you," I mumbled. One man clapped and a second followed after he heard the other start. The doctor moderating the discussion thanked me for sharing and asked, "Who would like to speak next?"

I wanted a drink right then, something cold to soak the ache. I needed to talk to Odie.

But I never called her and never left. I hung on for the entire month and it was the same routine every day: eat, shower, work out at the gym, call my mother, and go to classes and meetings. And there came a point during those group discussions where I'd stand up in front of the group and improvise whatever came to mind because no one cared what I said. Thinking about this now, I imagine all I wanted was for them to listen, to like me. "I once saved this blind man from walking into an oncoming semi, and I was as high as the moon on meth." Or, "You see these front teeth; they're all caps, 200% fake. Tyson stamped me in the grille one night after I told him he was only a small-time champ. Though I swear on my mother, I didn't feel a goddamn thing. I was too damn drunk on a dozen dirty martinis, at least." And, "One time I went down to New Mexico to train the ponies. Racing horses, what a fucking kick. And I was there for three months, got married, divorced, and met this other lady with three tits, swear to shit, and I fell in love with her too, not because of her rack, because she was nice and sweet, though I'm not going to lie I did get a peek at all three and they were quite nice, too."

Rehab doesn't fix you. When you're ready to get better then maybe, and only maybe, that's when it happens.

So one night, the second week there, when we broke for dinner I met this dark thin man named Jerome, who walked around all day bracing a bible. I'd heard from the others that he liked to read passages aloud from his bible while he walked you through the courtyard. I remember those spaghetti limbs, that billowy white beard. This man had been born a thousand years ago. He was my savior, or it was through him that God brought me back. Normally, I wouldn't give in to that voodoo jazz, but I was sold, through and through, as I was desperate enough to believe in anything.

The first time Jerome and I spoke he asked me, "Do you want to be saved?"

"I do," I said.

He pulled me aside. We stood under this towering pine tree. I remember thinking something terrible is about to happen. Or maybe I just hoped that something terrible would happen when he grabbed my arm and demanded, "Devil, come out of this man's body, now!" He started to convulse, one hand grasped the bible, and the other now reached and scaled the sky above. "Devil, come out of this man's body!" I felt my body shake. I keeled back, everything went black.

Now that was the first and only time in my life that I'd passed out, and when I did, some man, some crack-head who was also resurrected by Jerome, was waiting behind me to catch my fall. But I'm telling you, again, before this, I've never believed in any of this Jesus crap. Yet I was saved, an old tired soul born anew, swaddled into the arms of the unknown, the world went soft, the rustle of surrounding trees, blood thudded in my ear, ten thousand expressions at once. When I lifted my eyes I saw Jerome's pale blue burning eyes, his frothy atavistic beard, and I could hear this calm inner-voice tap inside my head: "Nobody gets hurt, nobody gets hurt, anymore."

50

ODIE QUITS HER JOB

Odie quit her job today. She came home a few hours early, just as I got home.

"What do you mean you quit?" I asked.

She put her bag on the kitchen table, kicked her heels off, and went to the refrigerator, pulling out a bottle of pinot.

"What do you mean you quit?" I asked again.

"I quit. What? I told you I was quitting," she said. "What's the big surprise?"

"You never told me that."

"No, Bernard, you just never listen. I've told you this numerous times. You're just never here. You're always somewhere else."

"I heard what you said. That you didn't like your job, and how you wanted to quit because you wanted to be with Madison. But we also talked about how we can't afford it. Do you remember that part? Why would you do something like this without discussing it first? We rely upon that money."

"Bernard, I don't want my life to be my job anymore. I want to raise my child."

"I understand. But these times don't allow for that. Honey, let's just talk about this."

"I already quit, Bernard." She poured herself a glass. "You're delusional, you know that? We spoke about this how many times? I told you how I thought it wasn't natural for a mother to be away from her child this much. You've lost it, Bernard. You really have. You don't listen to anyone. You don't listen to anything! You're always inside your own damn head. And wait we still haven't gone to see a doctor, right?"

She was probably right. I've been inside my head for a long time now, this book has taken over me, and I don't know what I've gained from it

"I listen. I listen to you. I've just been busy with the book, maybe."

She took a sip. "Oh, I forgot, you're going to write the next great American novel, right? My husband is going to be the next Great Gatsby."

"Gatsby is a character in a book." No one makes me angry like my wife.

"I know that. I know what I meant. And we can live off this great novel thing you're writing, right?" She smiled and finished her glass. Then she topped off another glass.

"It's a memoir. And you drink too much, these days," I said.

"Excuse me? *I* drink too much? And where do *you* get off? Listen, I've put up with your shit all these years. I think you can put up with mine."

"Oh, relax, already." And as soon as I said this, the drums started up, again. I knew she was going to flip.

"That's it. I'm going over there myself, right now." She took the last sip in her glass. "It seems my husband can't do the one thing that I ask him." She walked over to the door and began putting on her heels. "I guess I'll have to do it. If you want to get shit done around here, it seems you have to do it yourself."

"Odie?" I ran over to her. "Odie? Odie, just stop. I'll go." She put on her second heel, and I grabbed her by the shoulders, and shook her. "Just sit down." She pulled away and sat on the floor, staring up at me. She looked like a little girl.

"You're not going to go. I know you, Bernard. I've known you too long," she pouted.

"I know you."

"I'll be right back."

I stood outside in front of the house, again, where the drums came from. Twenty minutes probably went by, and car after car passed, and I got a whiff of a barbeque in the distance, burning flesh of some kind. And I could hear the Yankee game playing on someone's TV, and I saw the lady next door part her curtains, look at directly at me, and then shut them.

I waited some more, when finally the front door opened. A young, slender man stepped a few feet from his door. "Can I help you?" he asked, looking confused and suspicious.

"Hi," I said.

"Can I help you, I said."

I didn't move. I was afraid I'd scare him. "Yes. Hi. Sorry to bother you. Is it possible you can lower those drums?"

"Excuse me?"

"You see, my wife just quit her job, and she just asked me if you could stop playing the drums."

"Excuse me?"

"Hi, yeah, so my wife just quit her job..."

"I heard you."

"Oh, thanks. I'm sorry to bother you. I'll just be on my way."

"Why are you standing in front of my house?"

"I was just wondering if you could lower the drums."

"So you asking that my eight year old boy stop playing his brand new birthday present?"

"I'm sorry. I know. My wife asked me to ask you. She can't concentrate with the noise."

"Buddy, do you have a family?"

"Yeah, I do. I just told you about my wife. And I have a daughter, too. You have to admit, the drums are loud."

"You must be out of your bird. I don't even know who are."

"Really, no one else has complained about this? It's constant."

"Hey buddy, go home and scratch your ass." He turned and went inside.

"Thank you. Thank you very much." I waved and walked away. The drumming continued, and for some reason just as I walked around my block it stopped. And so I wasn't going to tell Odie what actually happened.

When I got back to my house there was a note under my windshield that said:

> *Dear old boy,*
> *Please call me at your convenience.*
> *Or just stop by. That might be better.*
> *Yeah, stop by.*
> *Need to talk ASAP.*
> *Your friend,*
> *Bill*
> *PS: I have that coyote urine that I told you about.*

51

SUICIDE JUMPER, A DIRTY KNIFE, JEROME'S BROTHER

After that first awakening at rehab, I'd spent a lot of time with Jerome studying the bible, walking the courtyard. I felt free of what came before, no reservations, no worries. I told him about my father and how his loss left me asking the big questions.

"I wish I'd spoken with him on those last few days," I said.

"I'm sure of it."

"You ever feel like something is missing?" I asked.

"Sure. I think we all do sometimes," he said.

Slowly, we walked in circles. He held his hands behind his back. "You know, when I was a young guy, years ago, I saw my own brother get a knife pushed into his stomach. Right on the sidewalk."

I didn't say anything. I just shook my head.

"And for a lousy, stinking dollar. He bled right out onto the street. Everywhere. His eyes fell back into his head."

Jerome's eyes were glassy and faraway.

He continued, "And we were on our way home from school. Broad daylight out. And why this white man didn't stab me? Well, he didn't."

"Did he try to?"

"Nope. He just looked at me. A long look, like he was trying to hurt me with his eyes. And then I just started to scream like hell and then he ran off."

"Did they ever catch him?"

"Nope. Back then black people didn't run after white people. They still don't, if you ask me."

"So he got away?"

"Yep, he got off clean with his dollar bill and that dirty knife. The point is, after that, I wanted to kill every single person I saw no matter who they were. And I'd dreamt up the most horrible ways of doing it. I knew it was only a matter of time before I'd start slitting people's throats. I knew it."

I looked right at Jerome.

"Guilt kills, my man," he said. "It burns you like no other. And I couldn't go one more day knowing my brother was now up to his neck in worms, and here I was sucking up the fresh blue air. Shit, all I wanted to do was walk as far away from all of this as I could. I'd just keep walking until I couldn't turn around anymore. And maybe if I got lucky I'd end up in the desert. There was nothing left inside of me. I felt as ugly as the world around me."

"I know that feeling."

"Sure you do." He listened to me, and it made me want to talk.

"I hate feeling things," I said, looking at the ground.

"You know, I could've stayed right there on that sidewalk with my brother, and for good. But then both of us would now be dead. And what good would that have done?"

"Yeah."

"You can make your world however you see fit, Bernard. Remember that."

52

HOME & DRUNK

First drink in twelve years. Fifteen years since rehab, maybe. A bottle of Jameson. Just pranked the Pierre. Asked to speak to Hiro. Hiro picked up, I hung up. I think I spoke to Bill? If we did speak, I don't remember what we spoke about.

Midnight and I don't know what I'm doing.

Home and drunk.

Madison and Odie are in Montauk for the weekend, a mother-daughter trip. Odie's idea to spend more time together.

Hate that I'm happy right now.

Woke on kitchen floor, I can't tell Odie.

Woke on the porch, sun in my face.

Not a good father, today.

Guilt kills, burns like no other.

53

THE NEXT DAY

Odie said, "What'd you do this weekend?"
I said, "I worked on the book."
"That's all you did?"
"Yep, that's it. How was your weekend with Madison? You had nice weather, huh?"

I couldn't tell her the truth. She'd leave me. I swore to myself I wouldn't do it again.

Anyway, Odie wouldn't have understood. How could she, if I still don't?

54

AFTER REHAB

I just remembered now that sometime after rehab I went to see Jerome again. This time I stopped by his church to hear him sing and preach. The high ceilings and sharp flowers, the plain silence and that slaughtered cross; it was too much at first. The room was thick with rapt faces tilted forward in their pews, death's grip, waiting on every word Jerome had to offer. Here in God's house, they got all the answers, or at least the illusion of some solution. For the short while I hung around, I felt part of something more than myself. If I was lonely at least now I was alone with everyone else, I thought.

Jerome then thundered, "Find the forgiveness in your heart! And let Jesus into your life! And we shall be released! When you have love for yourself and you love Jesus then you can love all the people around you." His voice echoed in the cavernous space.

For all those years my mother begged, pleaded for me to go to the Sunday Mass with her, I always refused to go. And here I was now at the back of this stained-glass wonder, that deep-sea feeling, reciting prayers for everyone I knew just in case someone was listening. I didn't believe in God, but I could give into this bottomless feeling I was experiencing.

After my tenth Hail Mary, I bolted before the ceremony ended. I couldn't face Jerome. I was worried that he might not want to see me, that he'd think I wasn't "awake" any longer.

55

MY MOTHER

When I think of my mother, I want to remember more. Maybe she's in the kitchen, swaying to the summer radio. Or Isabella is in my mother's arms as I race down a slide.

I don't see anything else. I could fault the drugs and drinking, but that won't allow me to remember more.

There's no direct path to the past, I suppose.

56

GANGSTERS & A FAMILY DINNER

Before Odie let me back into my apartment, I'd spent some time at another apartment in Howard Beach. This place was beautiful. It had limestone floors, handmade furniture, marble columns, and a giant hot tub. It was "owned" by a friend of the family, someone my mother knew. What my mother didn't know was that the owner was a gangster who was serving time in jail.

During those couple of months, I tried everything to get Odie back. I called all the time and she'd hang up. And once I thought I heard another man speaking in the background, so I threatened to come over there. I also told her it was ridiculous that she was even staying at my apartment without me there. But she was fixed on the idea that we needed more time apart, and as weeks went by I knew that it was over. Sometimes I'd drive past the apartment, late at night, when I knew she was sleeping, circling around the block sometimes ten times in one night. And I'd always stop in front of the place and look at the little blue light that was left on in the kitchen window.

"Come on Odie, just come to the window."

She never came out and I never went up to the door because it was too painful. Those steps were a reminder of everything I'd done wrong. Plus, I thought if I went to the door it might jeopardize my chances of getting back with her.

So I went about my life, focusing on day-to-day things, distracting myself as best as I could. I'd get up, eat, go to work, come home to my apartment, eat, sleep, and start again. And this routine allowed me to move forward without coming apart completely, because I still preserved this naïve hope that we'd be together again, as long as I stayed sober.

Back at work, I was lifting bags, smiling my face off at the clientele, standing at my post, looking at nothing, again. I was dead inside. Too much of my life had unraveled. I'd given away my best friend. After work I'd just disappear into my apartment, and watch TV or just listen to the street sounds, imagining how other people lived their lives, how their lives might crumble too. I even remember standing in front of the bathroom mirror a few times, thinking of a hundred ways to kill myself. I'd convinced myself that the suicide jumper I had seen early that year was the only person with intelligence in this world. But each time I went to do it, I'd think of my mother leaned over my grave.

My mother was there for me the whole time. She was not only my mother but she was my best friend too. She'd call me two, three times a day, or she'd come over to cook dinner. She'd tell me about when Isabella and I were kids, when my father was alive, or sometimes we'd just watch a movie, but she'd always reassure me that Odie ask me back soon.

"Bernard, it'll get better," she'd say.

Even with this reassurance, I still felt I was a failure to everyone. Though, part of me wanted to tell my mother everything, about all the drugs, all the partying. But the truth isn't always worth telling, especially to someone who didn't deserve to suffer another living day.

"You can't sit around all day and do nothing. Let's go to the park," she'd say.

"Nah, not right now, Ma." I looked at her, and I could tell she was worried.

"Let's go get something to eat?" she asked.

"Okay, five minutes. Okay?"

One particular night, a couple weeks after I'd settled in, my mother and sister surprised me with a home-cooked meal. It was our first family dinner since my father died. They arrived with an armful of groceries, walking into the house with more enthusiasm than I'd seen in years. Within minutes, the kitchen was suffused with Haitian spices.

My mother reeled about the countertop preparing the dish, while Isabella set the table. "Just two minutes. You two go wash up. Dinner is nearly ready," my mother said.

We cleaned up and sat at the table before a steaming meal. There was an empty chair but no one said anything.

"Now this is a family dinner," my sister said.

"Absolutely," my mother added, smiling.

Despite their cheerful mood, they both looked at me with this questioning glare. Each gesture I made I felt as if I were being watched. I tried to eat as fast as I could.

"Thanks, Ma. You didn't have to do all of this for me," I said. It was probably the first selfless remark I'd made in years.

"Please, Bernard. I'm your mother. Is the pork okay? Do you want more? Here, give me your plate?" She was so pleasant but nervous.

I wanted to reassure my family that I was going to be okay, that I felt better sober, and that I missed Odie and my father. But I said nothing.

Isabella asked, "Do you have work tomorrow?"

"Yep," I said, swallowing half a plantain, while grabbing another.

"You're going, right?" my mother asked, as she cut her plantains into tiny pieces.

She smiled but I could sense her discomfort.

"Yep," I said, with my mouth packed with pork.

My mother said, "Bernard, don't talk with your mouth full. I thought I taught you your manners years ago. We don't talk with food in our mouth," she said.

I looked at her, waiting for her say something else, maybe to tell me to go to my room, when all of sudden she began crying into her hands, a quick, violent sob. Then she just stopped, as if she weren't allowed to show her emotions in front of her children, a consequence, I think, of her privileged upbringing. I realized right then how much I'd contributed to her unhappiness.

Isabella stood up and put her hand on my mother's shoulder. "Oh, Ma."

My mother tried to laugh through her tears. "I'm fine. I'm fine." She pushed away Isabella's hand. "Who wants more pork? I want a piece for myself." She stood up, hurrying to the countertop. "Bernard, I'm going to cut a piece for you, too. Isabella, do you want one? I'm going to take two." She laughed, again.

"I'll have one," Isabella, said, appeasing my mother.

"Bernard, are you going to have one?" my mother said.

"I'll have a piece," I said.

"Good, I'll cut you two," she said, cutting into the pork.

"Just one, Ma for me," Isabella said.

"Oh, don't be difficult. Listen to your mother. Bernard what time do you have work tomorrow? Is it early?"

"Early eight o'clock tomorrow."

"Oh, not so early. Bernard, I'm going to cut you three. You need the energy," she kept slicing. "You know we used to eat this all the time when we were kids. Your grandmother and grandfather made sure there was dinner every night. Every night as a family we ate together." No one is ever prepared for their family to disintegrate.

My mother was alone. Her husband was gone and her children were now too old for her to look after. When a person no longer feels like they have a purpose, when their role in life is ripped away from them, something like a death follows. My mother could no longer be the person she wanted to be. Too much had happened, too much had come undone, and if she wanted to go on living, she'd have to become someone else.

57

BILL WANTS TO PURCHASE A SNAKE

At the bottom of my driveway, I went to grab my newspaper when Bill shot out of his house with some urgent news. "You have no idea, old boy. I spoiled my girl once more." He was slurping a big red ice in between sentences. "I gave it to her twice in one night. I gave her my big ol' heartboner."

"You're a lunatic, man."

"So listen, I don't know if I told you this already, but I think I'm going to purchase a snake soon in the next couple of days. I've been inspired," he said, smiling with all his teeth.

"Well, that's an idea, I guess."

"You really think so?" His eyes sparkled. "Hey, man, not to pry again but you don't look so good. Have you been sleeping at all? And you know you were pretty damn wasted the other night when you called me? I mean, thanks for calling but you were drunker than a goat."

"Yeah, I had a couple of drinks."

"I thought you don't drink, old boy?" he asked, smiling.

"That's right. I don't."

"But that hotel stuff you were talking about the other night. Crazy stuff, man," he said, smiling.

I looked at him, hoping he'd just go away. "What did I tell you? Nothing bad happened."

"I said 'crazy' not 'bad.' We don't have to talk about it now if you don't want to." He smiled and then added, "Hey, did you hear that Mrs. Davis passed away a couple of days ago?"

"What are you talking about? She passed away?"

"Yep. She's dead. I read it in the paper. She died maybe three days ago? I went to the mass last night. I was wondering why you didn't show up."

"Are you kidding me?"

"Don't you read the newspaper? Or do you only watch the news, old boy?"

"I was just over her house last week setting up her tomato garden. So wait, are there going to be any more services?"

"There's one more tonight. Look at the newspaper. I'm sure it says it in there." I said goodbye and went inside to the kitchen to get the paper. Odie was at the table reading a magazine. I picked up the paper and there in the obituary section I found her name: *Diane Davis. Eighty-one years old. Her husband passed 2012. Survived by no one.*

There was no mention of services. No kids. What the hell was Bill talking about?

I looked up and Odie was staring at me. "What are you reading?" she asked.

"Mrs. Davis died."

She put her hand to face. "Oh my."

"There's no funeral though. Why is there no funeral? There should be a funeral." I hardly knew this woman, another quiet death. I felt this acidic taste rise in my throat.

58

LADY FAIRFAX & GOOD WEED

Three months after rehab, and Odie still wasn't answering my calls. I was a wreck. I couldn't pull it together at work either. Life had been one missed opportunity after another, and I began to think that maybe I enjoyed missed opportunities. I realized that up until that moment my life had been, and would continue to be, composed of a series of events that I had no influence over. I could only try to make better decisions.

The first decision I made was letting go of the linen parties for good. I had done it before, but this time there was a sense of permanence. Sure, I got invited a few times afterward to join the crew for another party but I started to give them a series of empty excuses:

"I can't. Just can't. Tonight's my sister's birthday dinner."

"I hurt my back jogging yesterday. I can't knock one out with this sore back."

"I'm on antibiotics for a tooth infection. There was some real nasty pus. So I can't drink tonight. If I can't drink then I can't bang. Thanks though."

There were other justifications and elaborations, and each one felt more artificial than the last, but it was all I could muster at that moment. Eventually, the crew's collective vision established me as an antagonist to their wild secret, and I could sense that their shifting opinion would endure, and there'd be no more second chances. I was officially ostracized from the crew, as they ceased talking to me altogether, and I watch the cold pleasure in their faces when they passed by without a word.

"Hey, Rocco, what's doing?" I asked.

He offered nothing in return, just that knowing look.

On occasion, I'd walk past Hiro or Philip, and they'd both look at me with that same furtive smile.

"Hey, Hiro."

Nothing.

They were pushing me out, I knew it.

"Hi, Phillip."

Nothing.

So each day I went in to work thinking it was my last. And how the hell I was going to get another job, I had no idea

I remember one day standing at the door, playing with my glove, rolling it up and down, thinking about my first day at the Pierre, when I first tried on that top hat, calling my parents from the bathroom stall. It seemed then life was something I could manage, something to look forward to. And even if I wasn't part of that royal class my parents had hoped for, I still had a job, a purpose. I was a doorman at one of New York City's finest hotels, making my way, paying my rent, feeding my face. And now I was going to be fired, and after losing my father, then Odie, well, I no longer felt like a person.

I was no one.

Fortunately, some of the other staff, the ones not involved with the partying, still engaged me, and we became better friends by default, because I had no one else to talk to, and I think perhaps they were interested in finding out what went on at all these rumored fuck-parties.

That's why Wayne, this hip red-haired cat, the caretaker of Lady Fairfax's suite, asked me one day to join him for a quick burn up in her place. He pitied me, I suppose, and I think he wanted to get the scoop on what went on at these linen parties.

"You want to go or not?" he said, smiling.

I couldn't say no. Any distraction from dwelling on Odie and my misery was inviting. Plus, I wanted to see what all buzz was about. I'd heard that Wayne would chauffer others around her palace, which was the swankiest real estate in the building, occupying the top three floors of the hotel.

"I'll go," I said. Yet, I knew there was a huge risk sneaking around the building during daylight hours.

"Good, you'll love it."

The ride up rattled me a bit, even though I kept reminding myself that I was with Wayne and nothing could go wrong. Plenty of people had taken this tour before, and many more would take it after me. However, when Wayne opened the doors I fell to my knees as if I'd seen God. "Holy shit, oh my, shit, Wayne."

It's embarrassing now to think how excited I became. And I'd felt this sensation many times before. Admittedly, I was young and hopeless. Though, if you saw this place you'd understand that maybe there was nothing hysterical about my reaction. Over the years, I'd seen hundreds of rooms in this hotel, each one more staggering than the last, but none as grotesquely beautiful as this one.

"Holy shit, shit-my-shit, Wayne." It was the sort of beauty that hurt to look at. With Wayne as my guide, I ran around all sixteen rooms on all three floors, checking every glittering detail: the grand diamond chandeliers above, the impossible floral entrance, the vast ballroom with the Sistine Chapel motif, the eight bathrooms with gilded washbasins, six giant master bedrooms, six wood-burning stoves, three kitchens, and the four terraces that overlooked the shamble of NYC and Central Park. There were heated marble floors inlaid with mother of pearl, elegant lambskin rugs, automatic lights, twenty-five foot high ceilings, and gold everywhere. If only I could speak to my father to let him know what I saw.

You're like a little kid," Wayne said.

"My father, I swear, would've loved this," I said.

"It's a good one. No shit about that."

We scooted onto the balcony and rolled a joint, two tugs and I was lit. The city glistened in the night sky. We smiled and passed that bone back and forth.

"Thanks man," I said. Wayne was what I needed, a stranger, a face to look at, someone free of judgment. "This is good. Real good stuff."

"What is?"

"It's just good to not have to think about things, that's all. And it's nice that you're even listening to me." I passed the joint back, holding the smoke in my lungs for as long as I could, my eyes were closed, and then I just released the air out of my chest. "Good weed, too. I'm fucking blazed."

I would learn to be okay, again, I thought.

"Primo shit, right? I've been smoking it all month. My son gets it for me," he said.

"I didn't know you had a boy." I blew out the smoke. "How old is he?"

"I think he's going to be sixteen this month. Fifteen or sixteen, some shit. He's in eleventh grade."

"Well, it's good weed, anyway." I took another pull.

Start again.

59

MY MOTHER

When I think of my mother, she says, "Bernard, don't talk with your mouth full."

She says, "Who wants more pork?" She stands up, racing toward the countertop.

"Bernard, I'm going to cut a couple of slices for you"

"One will be fine," I say.

"Good, then I'll cut two," she says.

60

FIRED & GOING HOME

A few weeks after visiting the Fairfax suite, I got a call to come down to the Human Resource office. It turns out Miguel, one of the security guards, informed management that I was in her room. When they confronted me, I didn't lie. I'd broken the rules, and I was fired. After all that I'd been through—the rowdiest of orgies, ripping through mounds of coke, gallons of booze, a city's worth of women—and just like that I was canned.

"Thank you," I said to the young woman behind the desk.

"You're welcome," she said, looking confused. She handed me an envelope, a letter confirming my termination.

To be honest, I thought it would've been more difficult to leave. I was just glad that this part of my life would be left behind. It was a strange gift of some kind. Some of the other staff members didn't understand why I walked away without a fight.

"Is this it?" I asked the girl.

"Yes, Mr. Montpeirous," she said. "That should be all you need, I believe." She was careful not to look me in the eye. "Have a good day," she said, smiling.

"I will," I said. I stepped outside the door and turned around to look at her once more.

"Is there something else, Mr. Montpeirous?" she asked. She seemed uneasy.

According to her, I was now abandoning our script. I should've just walked out that door.

"What's your name, Miss?"

"I'm sorry?"

"Your name? What is it?"

"Audrey, sir."

"That's a good name. Have a nice day Audrey."

After that exchange, I left the building. I never went back to say goodbye to Hiro or Philip or anyone else from the crew. Nor did they try to chase me down. Some years later, sitting at a bar, I heard from this other doorman that Jimmy died of AIDS, and Rocco quit the job soon after I left because he got caught stealing a diamond necklace and a pair of Nike sneakers from one of the rooms. I am not sure what happened to Javier or some of the others, and if I'm not mistaken Mickey called me a few months after I left to tell me his wife left him. She bolted because he'd lost all their money at the casinos. Mickey hasn't called me since. Apparently, Hiro and Philip still run the show over at the Pierre. And I'd bet they've kept up with the linen-parties. I mean, what would stop them? It was a lifestyle for them, or better yet, a way of existing.

When I walked through those glass doors for the last time, I knew if I ever wanted to settle things in my mind I'd have to get Odie to at least to accept my apology. I walked down the block and caught a taxi to my old apartment, where Odie was staying, and offered the driver a few extra bucks to drive as fast as he could. The city rolled by the window, and it felt as if we'd traveled all night. When we finally pulled up to the apartment, I told the driver to just pull away. "I made a mistake. I'm supposed to go to Howard Beach," I said. I needed to leave Odie alone, I thought. If she wanted my company she would've asked.

The cabbie said, "Guy, you gonna need to make up your mind. You know if we go there it's gonna cost you twice the fare."

"That's okay. I can pay."

He turned the corner and went down to the next red light. As we idled, I saw him shaking his head in the rearview mirror. Across the way, there was this boy running along the sidewalk. He was racing after something. He had his pointer finger out in the shape of a gun and was blasting away his own "invisible" monsters. He turned the corner and disappeared around the bend.

"I have to get out," I said, as I opened the door.

"Buddy, are you high or something?" he snapped.

"Can you pull over? Please? I need to get out."

The light went green and there was a Hummer behind us honking its horn.

"You need to relax. There are cars behind me."

"Can you just pull over? I need to get out. I'm not feeling well. I'm sick. Here take your money."

"What's wrong with you?"

"Can you please just pull over?"

I looked out the window, at the passing buildings, and light crept through the gaps as people raced by, when I whispered, "You bend to look under the bed, and then it's on to the closet where all the linen hangs. Next it's in the bathroom, behind the shower, and then below the bed again. I don't see any monsters. I think we can all sleep now."

"Who the hell are you talking to?" His eyes narrowed in the mirror. "You're one fucked up dude," he said.

"You know what? Maybe I am. Maybe you're right. But you still shouldn't speak to people that way. My father drove a taxi his whole life and he would never talk to people that way," I said.

I then pulled out two twenties and overpaid the man, got out of his cab, and ran down the block. I almost knocked over an old lady carrying a grocery bag.

"I'm so sorry. I'm sorry." I walked backwards and then ran up the front steps to my old apartment. I knocked on the door as hard as I could. Odie didn't answer. I banged a few more times. She didn't come. She should have heard me. So I sat on the steps, waiting.

I didn't realize where I was when this police officer with a scraggly mustache woke me.

"What are you doing there, guy?" the officer asked.

I tried to gather my thoughts.

"Where are you supposed to be right now?" he asked.

"Here. This is my apartment." I pointed to the door behind me.

The officer just smirked, his arms folded over his belly. "Where do you live?" he asked.

Behind me the door opened and Odie appeared. Her eyes were raccoon black and she had on my flannel pajamas.

"Miss, do you know this man? He says he lives here," the officer said.

"Yeah, it's okay. He's not doing anything wrong."

The officer laughed to himself, and then he left, strutting down the block. Before Odie could close the door, I pressed, "Odie? Can I talk to you?"

"Bernard, what are you doing here?"

"Odie, I know I fucked up, I know this. But I didn't, I didn't mean for it to go this way.

You think I like being me? "

Folding her arms, she looked at me with a suspicious eye.

"That doesn't make any sense, I know. Look, I'm shaking. Look at my hands, both of my hands." I held up both of my hands. "Look, that's how nervous I am. That has to tell you something. I hate being me, Odie."

"I hate you, too," she said, her eyes welled up. She opened the door some more. "I hate you so fucking much."

I walked toward her and wrapped my arms about her body, almost breaking my arms.

"Bernard, not like that. You're hurting, you're hurting me."

I eased my grip and took a step back. She was beautiful and sad. The girl I met at the park that day was gone.

"Sorry, it's just been too long. What's it been? It's been three months, right?" I said.

"It's less than two months," she reminded me.
"Well, that's a long time."
"It's not that long."
"Okay, you're right. But to me that's long," I smiled. I looked at her, a long pause.
"Oh, and I'll buy you a new hairdryer this week."
"A hairdryer? What'd you do to my…?"
"I'll get you a new one tomorrow, actually."
"Bernard, what did you to my hairdryer?"
"I threw it out the window. But that was right after you punched me in the throat.

Do you remember when you punched me in the throat, too?"
"You're an ass."

I smiled and reached for her hand. She smiled back, a strained grin.

61

MY FATHER

I bring the chair closer, leaning into that soft breath that exits his lips:

> *We came to rest in front of this hotel. I forget which. At that point you'd let me get out of the cab and walk around a bit just as long as I didn't go off too far. I knew our address in case we separated.*
>
> *Dad, do remember that damn toothpick you chewed on every day? You told me you chewed on it so you didn't smoke your pipe as much? The customers wouldn't appreciate the smell in the cab. We'd lose tips. But that damn pipe too. You'd have me fetch that thing in the house almost every day.*

You fall asleep but I go on…

> *…there were two thieves. What was I 8 or 9? I saw them take that money out of your front pocket and I told you. You ran after them and caught them. Well, the police officer grabbed them as you chased after them. But I was your hero that day, you said. You said you needed me there that day.*

From the window, I watch the crowd shake by the streets, a haze of faces, when I look back at you, receding into the bed. I look out onto the street again, then back at you. You're now standing in the middle of the room. You start to dance, a dangle of bones no different than a puppet, as you try to impress me or to make me laugh, that same absurd face, and yet you don't know how to dance, so you just sit down on the tile and laugh into your hands. You stand up and look at me and say, "Where are the monsters?"

"I don't know," I say, my voice scratches.

You bend to look under the bed, and then it's on to the closet where all the linen hangs. Next it's in the bathroom, behind the shower, and then below the bed again.

"I don't see any. I think we can sleep now."

I smile.

You sit back down onto the floor and close your eyes. I sit next to you and hold your hand, a child's grip. Mom and Isabella walk back in. We hold each other. We're right by you. There's pressure under my left ear, I can't help but wince.

Everything spiraled back, the sun poked through the window slats. From my bed, I could hear Madison and Odie eating at the breakfast table. If I were wrong before, now it didn't matter. Somehow the smallness of my life, my family, gave it purpose. I ran downstairs into the kitchen to where Odie and Madison sat.

I said, "Odie, I want to talk to someone. I want to talk. You're right."

She laughed and looked at Madison, who was scooping up cereal. "I don't know what you're saying," Odie said. You could tell she thought I was crazy but something told her to show concern.

"I just don't feel good, Odie. You were right. I just had the weirdest dream."

"Bernard? I'm sorry. I don't mean to laugh. I just don't know what you're talking about, babe? You're mumbling."

"To go see that analyst person."

I made an appointment the next day and met with a Dr. Vasicek. He was a nervous man in his forties. He had keen blue eyes, the trust was immediate.

His first question was: "So what do you want to talk about?"

"I have no idea."

62

MY MOTHER

When I think of my father, I think of my mother.

63

REVOLVING DOOR

My younger days now seem to be without purpose other than being young and foolish. If nothing else these recollections have informed me of the gravity of life, my family's life, and how tenuous things can be. Without the pain of the past, I don't think I'd be able to appreciate all that's apparent, that life can be good, was good, and for that matter I can't regret anything that's come to pass.

Yesterday, Odie brought Madison up to the Roosevelt Hotel for a visit. Madison had off from school one day and begged my wife to see where I worked. She *had* to see her "Daddy's hotel," and she's told us last week that one day she's going to be a doorman too or a "door-*woman*" as she put it.

When they arrived, we decided to take a walk around the block, to give Madison a tour of the neighborhood. There was a cool spring breeze, and I did everything to provide Madison with that same New York experience my old man once offered me. Coming from me, though, it felt stilted. I was too self-aware of the "fatherly role" I was striving to inhabit. I could never be my father, even as I tried, "Madison, this is… and that is…" That New York beauty my father once embellished, and the gluttony I survived through all the nineties, was gone. That was so long ago. New York is something else now. And I don't know what it is.

"Daddy, can we *please* see your hotel now!" Madison asked, pulling at my leg.

"Sure, kiddo."

"Can we look at every room in the whole place? I want to see all the rooms, please!" "We can see a lot of them."

It was the first time Madison had seen this kind of luxury, and I could tell she was overwhelmed by the grandeur of the place, the old world décor, which of course brought on a slew of questions. I told her how it was built in the Roaring 20s at the peak of the jazz era.

"What's jazz mean, Dad? Can we see more rooms?"

She wanted to take a tour of the entire building, and with each new room it invited more awe, more curiosity. We went to the pool, the café, the ballroom, up and down the hallways, on over to the gym, where we stood outside looking in through glass at all of the people exercising, running, cycling, going nowhere, when Madison asked, "Why are all those people running and riding on those bikes?"

Pointing at the glass, I said, "It's called self-preservation. I think they all think they won't ever die if they keep this up."

Odie let out a stifled laugh, "That's ridiculous, Madison. They just want to be healthy. Don't listen to your silly father."

Madison looked at Odie with a knowing glance. A new closeness was forming between them since Odie had quit her job. It was nice to see Odie happy.

"You've got a good Mom," I said to Madison.

Odie grabbed my thumb, and they both flashed a smile.

We went back to the lobby and Madison sprinted toward this painting, an old realistic portrait of some grim-looking official with distinct, sharp brushstrokes, a somber overtone darkened by time. She reached up to put her hands on this canvas.

"Madison, you can't touch that sweetie," I said.

"Why not?" she whined.

"Just listen to your father. Come here kiddo."

She dragged her feet back to us. "Daddy, are all doormen the rich people?" she asked.

I looked right at her and then my wife.

Odie then said, "Madison, tell Daddy what you got on your social studies test."

"I got a B minus."

"That's really good news, Madison."

"The test was easy though. Everyone else got good grades too. My friend Lisa got an A, I think."

"Well, I'm still very proud of you."

"She's been working really hard," Odie said.

"Daddy, can I be a rich doorman one day, too?" Madison asked.

Draping my arm over her shoulder, I said, "Well, if things keep going the way they're going then there's going to be no doormen left. I bet soon our jobs will be replaced by robots."

"Robots? Does that mean the robots will take your money? Are we going to be poor,

Daddy?"

"You don't have to worry about that now. You've got a good family and that's all you..." I don't know if she heard me because before I could finish she ran off toward the lobby's revolving door.

Odie looked at me, smiled, and said, "She's just like you."

"You wish," I laughed, and looked straight at her and said, "I'm sorry for the shit I put you through."

"What are you talking about?"

"I was an asshole."

"Why are we talking about this again?"

"I'm not sure. But I'm sorry."

"How many times can you say sorry? I thought we said we'd put it to rest."

"It just wasn't me then. Well, it was but..."

"Bernard, please, already."

Madison pushed the glass as hard as she could, as if she wanted to break through it, and began circling around the door, over and over again, a twisted blur.

"So do you want to go Italy?" I asked. "I'll go to Italy if you want to go to Italy."

64

MY MOTHER

When I think of my mother, I think of Odie, Madison's mother, and how she should be dead. After Odie's third miscarriage, she almost bled to death giving birth to Madison, which is something I haven't thought about in years. I guess I was never interested in resurrecting that feeling, that image, or maybe I just wasn't brave enough.

When Madison and Odie finally came home from the hospital, I remember that first night at the apartment, how charged with meaning everything felt. The apartment appeared brand new. My voice felt strong, words and ideas came readily. During those first couples of weeks, our families were in and out all the time. There were dinners, lunches, and table talk, and everyone was listening to each other. Everyone was too happy to think about anything else but what was happening right then, right now.

"Can I get anyone something to drink?" I asked everyone. "We have orange juice, water, I don't know what else."

A few weeks after, as things settled in, the idea of being a father slowly became less abstract, and there was this distinct moment where I felt a release, just as I cradled Madison in my arms, tracing the contours of her face, her little hands, and those soft feet. That small heart clapped in her chest. Her eyes locked tight. The sound of her lip smacking and Odie's tired smile. To be a father felt close, new. But with this newborn intimacy came an unexpected anxiety. A hidden dread that this, all of *this*, could go away, would go away, and I'd be as I was before. I knew, I know, how easily emptiness circles back.

65

BILL

Bill stopped by and I told Odie to tell him I was in the shower. I ran into the bathroom to turn the water on. When I heard her say goodbye to Bill I came back into the kitchen.

"What did he want?" I asked.

"He said it was 'real important.' Something about a snake he bought? What the hell snake is he talking about? He dropped off this, too." She handed me this small plastic container filled with a blackish liquid, wrapped in a red bow. "He said that it's coyote urine. And that it's a gift."

"He's absurd. The guy acts like a cartoon or something."

"So why is this guy dropping off coyote urine?"

"Exactly. How should I know? He's crazy."

"He said to call him back after your shower."

"I'm not calling him back."

"Then I'm sure he'll call you back."

66

DR. VASICEK & LOST MEMORIES

When I'd asked my analyst, Dr. Vasicek, if I could go back to the Pierre Hotel, to say hello, he said it wasn't a bad idea.

"It might even be a good thing," he said.

Last week, I sat in his low-lit office and broke down for an entire session. It was the first time I'd cried like that in a long time. We talked about everything: my childhood, my family, the Pierre, those strange dreams, Madison, Odie, cocaine, the book. It was the conversation I should've had with my father or at least something like it, I thought.

"I'm not good at getting things right," I said.

"Why do you say that?" Vasicek asked.

"I'm just not."

But Odie was right. I needed to talk to someone. The more I spoke, the more I wanted to, and the more I realized I never did and still don't know how to.

Dr. Vasicek and I went on to speak about my father, my relationship with the old man. I told him about our taxi cab rides together, how I stole the cab, the dinners, him working too much, and I then remembered this one time when my old man scolded me for not catching a baseball. I was eleven and he called me a "pussy."

"He said it twice," I said.

"How did that make you feel?"

"Well, the second time hurt just as much as the first," I said.

Before this session, I had no recollection of this interaction. Though I don't think I wept in his office because of what my father said to me; it was more because I'd buried this memory.

We then spoke about the time my best friend was killed riding his bicycle. We were thirteen and I was right there as he was hit by that van, and I hadn't thought about this in years. Another session, I recalled walking along the beach with my father, not saying anything unless he did. Or the nights I read in bed with a flashlight when I should've been asleep for hours. And how until age nine, I was confused about whether I was black or white. Or when I was in grade school, I thought God had to be smarter than all people. Then in high school I abandoned my faith altogether. At twelve years old, I drank my father's beer when he wasn't in the room. Then there was Rodney King getting mauled on national television. So much more of it came back. How many other memories were lost memories?

"Sometimes one memory will trigger another memory that you would've completely forgotten otherwise," Vasicek said.

Dr. Vasicek also said it was *very* human to "tuck away" these memories that we can't handle, especially if we associate guilt with them. I now wanted to know what else I'd "tucked away."

After our session, he walked me to the door and put his hand on my shoulder. There's a distinct pleasure derived from a stranger's compassion, something I hadn't been open to for most of my life.

"Don't try to organize these memories just yet. It's enough just to acknowledge they exist."

"Well..."

"Well?"

"Well, that's what I thought I was doing with this memoir-thing I'm writing. I just write things as they come, and then I figure I'll make sense of the mess I make later on." "And?"

"And what?"

"How do you feel?"

"I don't know. It's just first draft. I don't know if it'll ever be done. It keeps getting interrupted. And I still have to revise many of my thoughts. It'd be nice if I could revise my life."

"Ha! We both know we can't do that. And there's no repeating this life either," he said, laughing. "So how'd you feel after writing this book?"

"Why do you keep asking me that question?"

"Don't you have any feelings regarding it?"

"You want to know how I feel? Honestly? Confused. More confused than before I started writing this damn thing. The more I try to remember the more I realize I've forgotten. This is first time I've ever looked inside myself like this. I'm just used to looking out, looking at other things, not myself."

He smiled, putting his hand on my shoulder, again. "If it makes you feel better, you're not the only one who's confused." He then stepped away and looked right at me. "We're all confused, Bernard. And that's not a bad thing. I think maybe you can even learn from it a little."

67

BOY

As a boy I cried into my pillow because I didn't want to die. It wasn't fair, I thought, that everyone I knew would die one day. I was seven or eight or nine, who knows, but I dreamt night after night of everyone leaving for good.

Now more than thirty years later, and though I might not be soaking through my pillowcase, I can't say that my fear of death has fully dissipated. Last year, I remember riding on an airplane during a summer storm, the sky was sharp green, and after some intense turbulence I became consumed with the images of a horrific plane crash. The screams, the fire, the final thoughts, and after we landed safely, I remember thinking that my childhood anxiety was still somewhere within, waiting for the "right" moment to spring to life.

If anyone ever says they're not afraid of dying, I wouldn't trust another word they say.

68

VISITING THE PIERRE

This morning I visited the Pierre Hotel. My old friend Javier, the dancing prince, stood at the front desk. He had sleepy eyes and this constant smile. I said hello and asked him if he remembered me.

"I do," he said, but he wasn't convincing.

This was the same Latino kid who I cavorted around million-dollar homes with our balls slinking about. But now after fifteen years he forgot who I was. I had to wonder how many others from the crew had put the past out of their minds.

"You don't remember partying together?" I asked.

He laughed. "Yeah, those were good times. Were you a doorman?"

"Yeah, that's..." I said Javier interrupted, "Yeah, that's right but I forget your name. Joe, right? Joey or something?"

"Bernard."

"Bernard, that's right. Not Joe. Bernard." His eyes searched my face for an expression, a reminder. "Are you dog-dick?" he asked, smiling.

I looked over my shoulder. "Yeah, that's me. Dog-dick. You remember that out of everything?" I looked over my shoulder again. "Hey, is Hiro still here?" I asked. "Yeah. I can call him for you." He picked up the phone.

"Nah, nah, that's okay. Just ask him if he's still got that blue peacock hat?"

Javier smiled right into my eyes.

I added, "Actually, don't tell him that. Just tell him I say hello."

He laughed. "Okay, I'll tell him."

A couple walked in, trailing behind five or more suitcases arranged on a carrying cart. A young doorman's head popped out from behind the stack. This man pushed ahead, grinning, asking all the right questions to the guests. "Is there anything else I can get for you, Mr. and Mrs. Hannah?"

Javier looked at the incoming customers and said to me, "I'm going to have to take care of this. Sorry to cut you short. But it was nice chatting. And I'll be sure to tell Hiro you said hello."

"Thanks."

69

ISABELLA CALLS, BILL, MY MOTHER, & THE GREEK GUY

After visiting the Pierre, I drove home in thick traffic to an empty house. Madison and Odie were at the beach and would be home later.

When I walked through the front door, I drifted through the house. Each room was cool and silent: the telephone sat on the cradle, the stillness of the bookshelves, the papers on the desk, the plates and pots and pans. It felt as if no one lived here.

I sat on the couch for maybe a few minutes when Isabella called:

"Hi Bernard," Isabella said.

"Hey."

"Are you busy? You sound busy."

"No. I just got in."

"Where were you?"

"I just went for a walk." I don't know why I lie. I should've told her I went to the Pierre. "How about you?"

"I'm just coming from Mom's."

"That must've made her happy."

"Yeah, I was there for only a little bit. I wanted to stay longer but I couldn't. She's getting old, really old. It's not easy," she said.

"Yeah, I spoke to her yesterday. I'm supposed to go over soon. I had to cancel plans with her a couple weeks back."

"She kept talking about Dad, all morning."

"That's nice."

"Yeah, I don't know. It was nice. But it also wasn't. Sometimes she doesn't have the nicest things to say about him."

"Yeah, she's mentioned some things to me recently, too. I don't get it. It's uncomfortable. Do all old people do that?"

"I know. She never used to do that. It must be that your mind shatters as time goes on. Or you just stop caring what other people think. Because that's not how I remember things. And I just don't think she should say stuff like that even if it is true. Dad was good to us."

"I agree."

"I still think about him all the time."

"Yeah, me too," I said.

"I guess what else is there to think about?"

"You're right."

"I hate that day." Her voice thickened. "I wish he was still here."

"I try not to think about it."

"Me too."

She laughed a little, coughing through her tears, and said, "Do you remember how hard you kicked that nurse? That poor lady."

"Kicked what nurse?"

"I don't know what nurse. The nurse, the one you kicked in the shin," she said.

"What are you talking about?" I took a moment to think, recalling a dream I had where Isabella kicked the nurse.

"Bernard? You there?"

"Yeah, I'm here. I didn't kick a nurse. I dreamt that. But I don't remember telling you that."

"Are you being serious? Or are you just screwing with me because of that conversation we had a few months ago about us going to the zoo."

"We never went to the zoo, Izzie. I know that for a fact. And I sure as hell never kicked any nurse. I mean, in my dream *you* kicked a nurse, but that was a few months ago."

I remember that. But I never kicked a nurse."

"You're saying I kicked this nurse in your dream now? You really don't remember when the nurses had to carry you out of his room. And you walloped one of them right just as they were taking you out of there. You were so upset."

"Izzie, what are you getting at? I told you I remember the dream with you and that's all."

"I'm confused. We've talked about this before, Bernard. Why are you playing dumb?"

"Seriously, now you're making me feel like I'm crazy."

"You don't remember crying that day, Bernard? I'm not trying to be mean."

"I actually remember not crying. That's what I remember."

"Come on! You wouldn't let go of him. You were sobbing. I felt so bad for you."

"Are you trying to fuck with me? Like I said, I'm not sure of what you're talking about. And what does this matter now anyhow? That was years ago."

There was an extended pause. I didn't want to talk anymore. I could hear her smacking her lips and it bothered me. "Dad never wanted to die," she said. "He told me toward the end that he was so afraid of what was to come. He kept saying, 'I don't want to die. I don't want go yet.' He'd say it all the time. I hate that day. I hate hospitals now, too."

"He never said that to me. Or maybe I don't remember that too." The truth is I don't recall any of it: the wake, the funeral, the months afterward, and I've never been able to admit this.

"Would you want to go to the cemetery with me next weekend to see him?" she asked.

"Yeah, perhaps, I'm not sure though. I'll have to see. I have to see what Odie has planned, or if Madison has anything too. There's a birthday party it seems every week with this one. But I'll try." I wasn't going. I knew it. I was lying. I can't go near it. I haven't been there since we buried him.

"Okay. Well, let me know. I'll clear out a day this weekend and we can go. I'm busy this weekend too but I can try to make room."

"All right then, then call me during the week. I'll talk to Odie. Okay? It was good talking to you."

"Bye, Bernard."

We hung up and I slammed the phone down. I walked out into the backyard and sat on the deck and began following the sky, that great blue dome that hovers overhead. A lawnmower ran a few backyards away. I couldn't think straight. And that kid was playing those damn drums again. "What the fuck!" I punched the side of my house. A frog now leapt across grass, diverting my attention, as he attempted to hop up onto the deck. He fell but tried again as if he hadn't failed the first time. By the second try he was leaping right beside me. He then decided to jump back onto the grass. In the distance, the train's engine cut up the expanse. I could hear my neighbors in their backyard bickering about where to put their Butterfly Bush: "Over here, so when we have guests they can see it." "No it won't get enough sun there." "Yes, it will. Just put it over here. I'm not arguing with you." "So don't argue then." "I said I'm not going to argue with you."

I wanted to scream. I went inside and poured a glass of orange juice and then dumped it down the drain. I went into the living room and sat on the sofa. I went outside to make sure I didn't leave anything. I walked into the living room and sat on the chair by the window. The curtain billowed in the breeze. I followed its movement: slow, deliberate and graceful. I stood up and hurried upstairs to the office. I took out that family photo, the one with the Davy Crockett hat. I ripped it into pieces. I ran downstairs to call Odie, and then decided not to. I went outside to go for a walk.

Bill was out front washing his truck, when I think he said, "Where you off to, old boy? You never called me back. Did Odie tell you I stopped by when you were in the shower? Did you get the coyote urine?"

He walked toward me, paralleling my stride.

"Yes, I got it. Thanks. I'm just going for a walk," I said.

"I tried calling you a few times, old boy. Something wrong?"

"Nothing's wrong."

"Are you having those dreams again?"

"What are you talking about?"

"If it's the dreams, I can listen if you want."

"Who told you that?" I looked him right in the eye.

"No, one, I read it in your book."

"What are you talking about, Bill? You read my book? What book? I don't have a book."

"Okay, I lied. But don't lie to me, old boy. You told me all about it when you were drunk the other night. You know that Hotel you worked at sounds wild." He smiled at me, and said, "I still can't get over the fact you ate a Twinkie out of a girl's ass!"

"I didn't tell…tell you that," I stammered, increasing my pace.

"Some of it's still hard to believe. I have to admit you're a sick bitch, old boy. But you're also my hero, now, too. Oh, and don't worry, I won't make a peep about any of this to Odie. Nor will I mention anything about you getting boozed up the other night. You've got my word."

I walked even faster. "I've got to go now, Bill."

Bill tried to keep up. I'd never seen him move so fast. His belly rocked with each step. "Can you please slow down for minute, old boy?"

"Bill, I can't talk now."

He huffed, his legs wobbled. "Please, listen, now I need to tell you something very important, sort of devastating, actually."

"I can't right now."

His face darkened and he raised his voice. "Now I listened to your whole goddamn story, and so now you're going to listen to mine there dog dick."

"Bill. I'm just not feeling like myself. Can't it just wait? Did you just call me dog dick?"

"No it can't. I said it was important. My girlfriend left me. Jenna left me. She hated the snake idea. She hates snakes, she said. She's afraid of snakes. Now why would you encourage me to do try this with her?" he might've said. I couldn't hear him that well. I was trying to walk as quickly as possible.

"Bill, I don't know what the hell you're talking about. I'm really sorry to hear that. I just can't listen to your life right now." He kept walking alongside me. I felt dizzy. I couldn't stop thinking about what Isabella said.

"She's just a young stupid girl. I know that. I made the mistake. But now my wife is getting married, too. And I just found this out about that slut. She's getting married. And now I don't know what I'm going to do with myself. I'm so fucking lonely. You think I like being me?" I think he said.

When I turned to look at him his face was covered in tears. "I promise we can talk about this later, Bill." I continued to out-walk him. I couldn't listen. The more I listened, the more it hurt. I can't listen anymore. Not to him or anyone.

"I knew it, old boy. You hate me, too. Don't you? I get it. Everyone hates me. I'm telling your wife what you did! I'm telling her you got drunk, too! I'm telling her everything!"

"Will you please stop, already? And stop taking everything so damn personal! I'll listen to you tomorrow. Okay, tomorrow, Bill," I think I said, as I moved faster, past some guy cutting his lawn with scissors, who waved as I went by. I didn't wave back. I started to jog. What's his name? Brian, Peter? I went faster. Isabella had to have been lying. I looked up. The sun pierced my eye. What am I doing? I don't know what I'm capable of anymore, what I'll do next. All those linen parties. They might as well be happening right now.

I'm no different. And there are things I've done that I can't mention anyone, I'm still too embarrassed for my wife, my daughter, and I'm sure there are others that I've wiped from memory. If I can't remember what I've done then who says I'm not going to do it again. If I can't remember things then maybe *nothing* ever happened. If I don't remember then I don't exist. I feel wrong. I feel like I'm five years old again. I'm afraid of everything. I want my father here. I want him to carry me back to my room so I'm safe again. This book, this memoir, these dreams are useless if I can't remember things as they were. And I can't help but be me. I was drunk the other night. What kind of father am I? What will happen next? Change is something that happens and only for the moment. We forget and start again, but only as ourselves, over and again. We think we're someone else and nothing happens, not until we die. And there I was standing in the middle of the street, traffic moving in either direction, as I darted in and out of a bramble of cars, an animal being shot at, over and again.

When I finally made it over to the sidewalk, I sat down on the curb in front of this strip of stores and called my mother.

"Ma."

"Bernard?"

"Hi."

"Is everything okay, Bernard?"

"Yeah, everything's fine."

"Oh, it sounds like something's wrong."

"No, nothing's wrong. I'm just saying hi. I wanted to say hi."

"When are you going to visit? I'd like to see my granddaughter."

"Maybe, tomorrow, Ma. I don't know. Ma, am I nice to you? I mean I think I am. I always thought I was. But do you think I've been good to you all these years? We talk, right?"

"Bernard, what kind of question is that? Are you okay?"

I held back my tears. "Okay, you're right. I know it's a stupid question." I kicked an empty Coca Cola can into the street. "But do you remember when Dad died? Of course you do. And you remember when we were in the hospital right before he passed? When Dad died did I cry? Was I crying in the hospital room? I don't know if you'll remember this."

"Bernard, why are you asking me this?"

Then I started to cry, my whole body shook.

"Nothing, Ma."

"Bernard, are you okay?"

"Yeah, I'm fine." The tears just came. "No Ma, I'm not fine. I mean I am. I'm fine. I'm just crying. I'm crying right now. Can you hear my crying over the phone? I never cry." I laughed through my tears.

"I miss Dad, Ma. I miss him." I clenched the side of my pants. "Am I even allowed to say that?"

Now a man in a muddy apron charged out of his store, 'Daedalus' Gyro.' This bald nut had caterpillar eyebrows and a nose that almost grabbed his chin. He shouted, "Get the hell off my concrete. You going to spook the customers! I call the police on you."

"Ma, hold on one second."

"Where are you going?" she asked.

"Just hold on, Ma."

By the time I covered the phone this jerk shadowed over me. I stood up and looked him cold in the eye.

"Get off my fucking concrete, you baby man," the man said.

"Excuse me, sir? Listen, I'm on the phone."

"You don't know me. I piss in your shoe, fat man. Now, get off my concrete now, I say!" he shrieked, laughing into his hands.

"You're out of your bird, man," I said to him. Then I said to my mother, "Ma, I'll call you right back."

My mother raised her voice: "What bird? Where are you going? Why are you getting off the phone, Bernard?"

"Just let me call you back. I'll call you back in one minute. There's this guy who's yelling at me."

"He's yelling at you? What do you mean he's yelling at you? Who's yelling at you?" "Not at me. He's not yelling. He's just asking for directions. Just let me go, Ma. I'll call you back in ten minutes."

"Okay, call me then. As long as everything is fine. In ten minutes. Call me back," she said.

"Everything's fine. I'll call you back. I'm hanging up," I said, and hung up.

The Greek man now had his finger in my face. A vein scribbled down his forehead.

"Get off the concrete!"

The lady from the video rental store and the fish market stepped outside to watch the commotion. They looked on quietly.

"Relax, man," I said.

He said, "I work too hard, too long in this country, for you to fuck me up! You're not to fuck me up! Now get off my concrete!"

"I'm not on your concrete, sir. This is a public sidewalk!"

A man and a woman walked out of a hair salon and stood smiling. The video rental lady and the fish guy walked over to the hair salon people and they all looked on together.

This Greek now jumped up and down. "You cry on my concrete, talk on my concrete. You Americans, talk, cry, talk, always talk, cry, talk, but say *nothing* on my concrete."

I grabbed him by the apron and I got right up in his face and whispered, "I was talking to my mother, sir."

"Fuck you, fat man. You weren't talking to the Ma-ma, dog dick. You were just talking to yourself the *whole* time," he said.

I let go of him and just walked away, heading for home. Odie and Madison would be home soon.

70

WHAT COMES NOW

I missed my father's death. I was there and nothing comes. No picture or dream or journal or conversation calls back that moment as it was. I've tried to circle back and recall what it was like, and some parts are there, some parts are made up, and others are just broken, missing as if they never happened. It seems what's *not* said in this book is just as important as what is. The real story, full story, resides in what's forgotten, hidden within the recesses of time. So how can I ever write something that's truthful to my experience, my life, when our poor memories won't permit it?

And I now know, after writing this book, I hardly knew my father at all, and never will. Time has eclipsed that possibility, and it might sound fatalistic, but I only have an idea of how he happened to be, a warm, sentimental understanding, and that's all. And I don't think not knowing, not understanding is the great sadness of my life or anyone's life— however detached that may seem—nor is the fact that I was unable to cultivate a meaningful relationship with the old man before he passed. No, I think the real sadness is that I was *always* afraid, all these years, to confront the elusive facts that made up my life.

Death shook me. My father's passing undid me. And so I stepped away from everyone, absorbed by a private madness even I wasn't fully aware of.

Yet it's only apparent to me now that this story, this book could've been about anything: a talking dog, a small town murder, an old pair of shoes, or just some fancy coke orgy and *still* it would've somehow reverted back to my father, my mother, my family. What was meant to be a book that explored the bombast of my youth has devolved into something else. The great parties of my past, however bold and irreverent they now seem, held no great weight after all. Your parent's death defines you, even kills you a bit.

This morning, after a pleasant family breakfast, I went to the old man's gravestone, to listen, the old man and me. I sat down crosslegged in front of his stone, the grass wet with dew, as light reached through the high oaks. I had nothing left. I just listened to wires humming above and surrounding traffic, when I saw this youngish blonde a few graves ahead, now perched over some lost loved one, gently placing a pink carnation to the ground. Her thin hand shook, her face torn with grief. I couldn't look at her. I closed my eyes as my mind carried over to a family dinner, almost forty years prior...

My father sits, his vibrant eyes, with Isabella bouncing on his knee, as she fools with a spoon, trying to steady it on her nose. Hovering over a pot of steaming pork and rice, my mother stirs with purpose. And I'm circling the table, round and round, shooting my rifle at the air.

My mother calls out, "Bernard, you've got to sit down. We need to eat before we go to the zoo."

I let off a shot into the air. "We're going to the zoo? We're going to the zoo! We're going to the zoo!" I sing and run to my seat. I clap and bang on the table, continuing with my song. "We're going to the zoo!" Isabella and my old man join in the song. "We're going to the zoo! We're going to the zoo!" Then my mother turns, her grin is real, lasting.

"Bernard, don't talk with your mouth full. I thought I taught you your manners years ago. We don't talk with food in our mouth," she says, when all of sudden she cries into her hands, a quick, violent sob. Isabella stands up, putting her hand on my mother's shoulder.

"Oh, Ma."

My mother tries to laugh through her tears. "I'm fine. I'm fine."

My father now sits, his eyes are clear. Isabella is propped on his knee, a spoon on her nose. My mother is cooking, and I've got my rifle, scampering around. There's a strange shine about everyone, as if their smiles say: everything is good, we're going to do this.

"Bernard, sit down. The zoo, we're going to the zoo."

"We're going to the zoo!" I shout, leaping to my seat. My mother turns, grins.

My mother pushes away Isabella's hand. "Who wants more pork? I want a piece for myself." She stands up, hurrying to the countertop. "Bernard, I'm going to cut a piece for you, too. Isabella, do you want one? I'm going to take two." She laughs. She cries. She laughs.

"I'll have one," Isabella, says, appeasing my mother.

"Bernard, are you going to have one?" my mother says.

"I'll have a piece," I say.

Again, Isabella has her spoon, and my dad smiles, and my mother stirs the pot for the family. We're going to the zoo. I circle the table, everything is good, a strange shine.

"Sit down, Bernard. Sit down. Sit."

"We're going to the zoo!" I shout, flying my pistol through the air, around and around the table.

"Sit down, Bernard. Sit down, Bernard. We're going to the zoo. Sit."

"We're going to the zoo!" I shout, over and again.

"Sit down, Bernard. Sit down. Sit. We're going to the zoo. We're going. Sit.

Bernard."

"We're going! We're going to the zoo!"

I don't care if this is made up. The more my mind plays the more real, the more meaningless it all feels, and I don't want to be anywhere else. I'm right here, here where I don't have to remember, where I can make things up as I go. Maybe I'll just remember my life as I want to remember it. Yeah, that's what I'll do.

I'll start again.

AUTHOR BIOGRAPHY

Bernard Montpeirous's first experience in the tourist industry was serving as "copilot" in his father's taxicab in New York City in the early seventies. While his father was waiting for his next fare, Montpeirous got to know doormen at upscale establishments in the city. On his father's advice, he later became one himself.

Montpeirous's career has taken him to some of Manhattan's oldest and most luxurious hotels. He spent seven years working at the Pierre Hotel and the last twenty years at the Roosevelt Hotel.

Made in the USA
Middletown, DE
20 September 2017